INSIGHT ● GUIDES

EXPLORE

MALLORCA

D0932337

⊙ Walking Eye App

Your guide now includes a free eBook to your chosen destination, for the same great price as before. Simply download the Walking Eye App from the App Store or Google Play to access your free eBook.

HOW THE WALKING EYE APP WORKS

Through the Walking Eye App, you can purchase a range of eBooks and destination content. However, when you buy this book, you can download the corresponding eBook for free. Just see below in the grey panel where to find your free content and then scan the QR code at the bottom of this page.

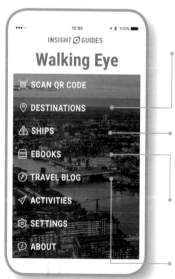

Destinations: Download essential destination content featuring recommended sights and attractions, restaurants, hotels and an A–Z of practical information, all available for purchase.

Ships: Interested in ship reviews? Find independent reviews of river and ocean ships in this section, all available for purchase.

eBooks: You can download your free accompanying digital version of this guide here. You will also find a whole range of other eBooks, all available for purchase.

Free access to travel-related blog articles about different destinations, updated on a daily basis.

HOW THE EBOOKS WORK

The eBooks are provided in EPUB file format. Please note that you will need an eBook reader installed on your device to open the file. Many devices come with this as standard, but you may still need to install one manually from Google Play.

The eBook content is identical to the content in the printed guide.

HOW TO DOWNLOAD THE WALKING EYE APP

1. Download the Walking Eye App from the App Store or Google Play.
2. Open the app and select the scanning function from the main menu.
3. Scan the QR code on this page – you will then be asked a security question to verify ownership of the book.
4. Once this has been verified, you will see your eBook in the purchased ebook section, where you will be able to download it.

Other destination apps and eBooks are available for purchase separately or are free with the purchase of the Insight Guide book.

CONTENTS

ART COLLECTIONS

Discover the wonders of Palma's top three art galleries (route 2), admire the extraordinary collection at a small-town train station (route 7), or marvel at the artistic interpretation of local wine labels (route 14).

RECOMMENDED ROUTES FOR...

FAMILY ADVENTURES

Take an alternative approach to kids' theme parks and head instead for Mallorca's extensive network of caves and grottoes (route 11), or kick back with a bucket and spade on the longest beach in the south (route 12).

FOODIE PARADISE

Shop for edible treasures at Palma's atmospheric delis and sweet shops (route 3), or pack a picnic of treats from local markets (route 13).

THE GREAT OUTDOORS

Snorkel the deserted island of Sa Dragonera off the southwest coast (route 4) and enjoy the slowed-down pace of Pollença life (route 8).

HISTORICAL LEGACY

Soak up Palma's Arabic provenance and old Jewish quarter (route 1), admire the ancient monasteries and sanctuaries of Mallorca's hinterland (route 13), or bag yourself a slice of old-fashioned mountain life (route 5).

LITERARY GENIUS

Discover the Mallorca of George Sand and Robert Graves (route 6), or find out how light and landscape equals poetry at the Cap de Formentor (route 8).

MALLORCAN ARCHITECTURE

Explore the ancient heart of Palma (route 1), or be dazzled by the extravagant decor of Sóller's Modernista mansions (route 7).

SURF, SAND AND SUN

Escape the crowds at some of the island's most hidden beaches (route 10), or join the cool kids on the strands of the south (route 12).

INTRODUCTION

An introduction to Mallorca's geography, customs and culture, plus illuminating background information on cuisine, history and what to do when you're there.

Village of Deià

EXPLORE MALLORCA

Often spoken of as the 'pearl of the Mediterranean', Mallorca lures with sun, sand and sea, but also has plenty of other charms to recommend it, from a cosmopolitan capital to a stunning interior made for active exploration.

Palma has more than enough to offer for an entertaining long weekend, but it's the 'other Mallorca', the road less travelled, that keeps people coming back for more. Whether you're looking for secluded sands or hip clubs to dance the night away in, remote country villages or soaring mountain tops, five-star golf courses or pristine diving in crystal-clear waters, the biggest of the Balearic Islands has something to suit everyone.

GEOGRAPHY AND LAYOUT

The Balearic Islands were formed nearly 100 million years ago when limestone bedrock was forced upwards, creating a peninsula jutting out to sea from the present-day Spanish coast around Valencia. Mallorca is the biggest of the four islands – Menorca, Ibiza and Formentera are the other three – and offers travellers a diverse landscape: long, sandy beaches and isolated rocky coves are framed by sapphire-blue seas and backed by dramatic mountain peaks, while olive groves and vineyards fringe the sparsely inhabited interior plains. Not for nothing is the island often referred to as the Spanish mainland in miniature. Mallorca may be the largest of the Balearic Islands, but it is not a big place. It has more than 550km (325 miles) of coastline, but at its widest point – Cap de Sa Mola in the southwest to Capdepera in the northeast – it is only 100km (60 miles) across; at its narrowest, from the Badia d'Alcúdia in the north to the Badia de Palma in the south, it is just half that distance.

Getting around

Mallorca makes for easy travelling, and the routes in this guide have been arranged to run clockwise around the rim of the island, starting in Palma and ending up in the centre. It is by no means exhaustive – there is still plenty to explore on your own – and hiring a car is advisable. Driving on the island is easy, and with the notable exception of the MA-15, which cuts across the centre, is generally fairly trouble-free in terms of traffic.

The main cities featured are easy to walk around, Palma included, and for routes 1, 2, 3 and 7 you can easily get around on foot or by public transport. Outside the towns there is a train network that runs from Palma to Sóller, stopping at small towns en route, and there

Fishing harbour of Sant Elm

is an extensive bus system. However, if using public transport you need to plan in advance and will need to allow extra time.

Walking paths around the island have been opened up and clearly marked, and a number of hilltop sanctuaries provide rest and respite for walkers; natural parks are widely promoted and user-friendly.

HISTORY AND ARCHITECTURE

Skeletal remains indicate that the Balearic islands were inhabited from as early as 4000 BC, but the oldest architectural ruins date from the 3rd millennium BC. The Talayotic Age that followed – from 1000 BC to the Roman conquest – left the most archaeological testimonies on the islands, the defensive stone structures called talayots, believed to have been built by a people who came from the eastern Mediterranean. The Carthaginians, whose occupation dated from the mid-7th century BC, recruited Balearic mercenaries whose slings were the terror of the Romans. It was not until 20 years after the destruction of Carthage (146 BC) that Rome was able to subjugate the islands.

The Romans settled in Mallorca, but had little interest in the island beyond using it as a stopgap on more important missions of conquest. It was really with the arrival of the Moors in 902 that it advanced in terms of commerce and agriculture, cuisine and culture, language and education. Under the Arag-

onese king Jaume II the island entered a 'golden age', when some handsome little villages sprang up in rural areas such as those featured in route 5, and heaps of money were poured into gentrifying the important towns and cities.

By the 15th and 16th centuries, however, the gap between rich and poor stoked the fire of civil unrest, which was manifested in endless uprisings, while prosperous towns like Palma, Sóller and Andratx lived in a constant state of fear of pirate attacks. Compounded by the arrival from mainland Europe of the plague, which wiped out a hefty chunk of the population, these were dark days for Mallorca.

Modernista Mallorca

By the time of the Napoleonic Wars (1799–1815) many islanders had cast in their lot and moved to the New World, seduced by the promise of gold. Wealth eventually came back in the form of the lavish Modernista (Catalan Art Nouveau) mansions of the island's main towns, coloured hydraulic tiles made famous by Huguet (www.huguet-mallorca.com), and the stained glass and whimsical wrought iron of the Belle Epoque. Travellers interested in architecture shouldn't miss routes 1 and 7, which feature many of the island's finest landmark buildings.

Boom and bust

Things were quiet throughout much of the 20th century – even the Spanish

Beach at Magaluf

Civil War (1936–9) didn't really reach Mallorca's shores – until, in 1960, the opening of Palma's Son Sant Joan airport to international traffic brought the first proper rush of tourists. This was in keeping with Franco's vision of turning great swathes of the Spanish coastline into tourist resorts along the lines of those he had heard about in Florida. Huge resorts like Magaluf and others along the east coast sprang up over the next 40 years, but the flow of foreign cash slowed – by the 1990s the island had managed to position itself alongside the Costa del Sol and Benidorm, with a reputation for dishing up a particularly virulent strain of mass tourism that put many people off coming.

The new Mallorca

Mallorca has never been a place to sit back and let things happen, and the early years of the 21st century have seen it smarten up its act considerably, in keeping with the needs of a more discerning traveller. Boutique hotels sprang up in Palma, and the tourist office stopped advertising sun, sea and sangria and started marketing *agroturismos* (smart rural hotels, often with a foodie focus), cycling holidays and a vast portfolio of cultural events. Even the budget airlines have come under fire from some tourism officials, who say they attract the 'wrong sort of tourist'. While that may be somewhat misplaced – it is not unheard of for millionaires to check in with easyJet, after all – 21st-century Mallorca is definitely a class act.

CLIMATE

Mallorca's climate is temperate most of the year, although it does get its wintry spells (even, on some occasions, snow in the high Tramuntana). November, December and January can also see many businesses on the island closed. July and August, by contrast, can get extremely hot and the hotels rammed. Generally, then, spring and autumn are the best times to visit, with balmy temperatures by day, cool evenings and fewer crowds. From January to March it can be wet, so if you're here on a hiking holiday, do come properly equipped.

FLORA AND FAUNA

The flora of the island is as diverse as the landscape. There are cultivated olives, almonds, apricot and citrus trees; holm oaks and pines flourish in mountainous regions, with rosemary, lavender and heather turning the hillsides purple. There are sturdy palm trees growing at sea level, and bougainvillaea brightening village walls; and there are wild orchids and water-loving reeds, sedges and poplars in the S'Albufera marshes.

Mallorca is rich in birdlife. Come in spring, as so many birdwatchers do, to see the numerous migrants who find Mallorca a convenient stopping-off

Modernista architecture   *S'Hort del Rei (King's Garden), Palma*

place. The Boquer Valley, near Pollença, is popular with those in the know. S'Albufera, on the north coast, plays host to numerous resident and migrant species, including the cattle egrets that can be seen standing on the backs of cows, pecking insects from their hides, and birds such as Eleonora's falcons that spend the summer here. Among the most colourful and exotic birds that can be seen in many locations in summer are bee-eaters and hoopoes. The island of Cabrera and the Parc Natural de Mondragó in the southeast corner are among the best places to spot migrating seabirds.

DON'T LEAVE MALLORCA WITHOUT ....

Going underground. Mallorca's landscape is packed with stunning caves and grottoes, a feature of the porous limestone of the Balearic Islands. The Coves de Artà are some of the most spectacular that can be visited. See page 66.

Savouring gourmet goodies. From sweet *ensaimadas* to New Mallorcan Cuisine, farmers' markets and freshly caught fish, Mallorca is a foodie's dream. See page 16.

Shopping 'til you drop. Whether you want designer labels or traditional arts and crafts, Mallorca has something to offer all tastes and budgets. See page 20.

Admiring the views. The west coast has some stunning scenery and the best places to take it all in are from the viewing points Mirador de Ricard Roca and Mirador de Ses Ànimes. See page 42.

Tasting the local wines. Wine has been made on Mallorca since Roman times. Today you can visit several winemakers, both modern and traditional, to sample the local vinos. See page 80.

Lazing on a beach. Mallorca's beaches are legendary, whether you are looking for the white powdery sand of Es Trenc or lying on a sunbed surrounded by beautiful people at the private Puro Beach. See page 71.

Getting away from it all. Escape from the crowds with a trip through the Serra de Tramuntana, a Unesco World Heritage Site, or book a stay in a mountain-top sanctuary. See page 44.

Visiting Deià. Famed for its potent mix of literary, artistic and celebrity heritage, Deià is a stunningly pretty village clinging to the side of a mountain. The home of Robert Graves, who wrote many of his novels here, is open to the public. See page 48.

Having a go at a water sport. From bumping over the waves on an inflatable banana to sailing, windsurfing and diving, there are water-sports schools right around the island catering for all levels. See page 25 and page 62.

Appreciating the art and architecture. Explore Palma's world-class art galleries and learn about the Modernista movement at Can Prunera in Sóller. See pages 35 and 52.

Basílica de San Francisco, Palma

POPULATION

The population of Mallorca is just over 859,000, nearly half of whom live in Palma. Compare that to the 10 million-plus tourists the island welcomes every year and you get a sense of just how hospitable your average Mallorquín can be. A sizeable chunk of the population is made up of resident expats (mainly British, German and Scandinavian). Mallorquíns are a generally friendly bunch – especially if you take the trouble to learn a few words of Catalan – and you will find them warm, helpful and welcoming, provided you respect their culture and environment.

Local customs

Islanders, with the exception of farmers in very rural communities, are bilingual, speaking both Mallorquín (a dialect of Catalan and the first language of the island) and Castilian fluently. In the main tourist areas you will find that many people also speak some English and German, and there is nearly always someone about to help should you find yourself stuck.

Do bear in mind that Mallorcan hours follow those of Spain: shops open around 10am, lunch is served from 1.30–3.30pm and dinner from 9pm onwards. You can drop in for a tapa and a glass of wine in any bar at pretty much any time of day, but many places are closed on Sunday night and all day Monday. The main museums are generally open all day (although many close on Monday), but smaller ones may shut for a siesta. And out of season (November to the end of January) many places close down altogether – which is great if you want an extremely quiet holiday, but something to consider if you have your sights set on a certain hotel or restaurant.

POLITICS AND ECONOMICS

Something of a political conundrum, Mallorca has no fewer than 35 political parties, each of which competes for a seat in the council of 53 municipalities. As of 2015, the autonomous government of the Balearic Islands has been formed by the left-wing Partido Socialista Obrero Español (PSOE), and the Més per Mallorca (MES), a coalition of small independent parties promoting ecological and left-leaning aims.

Tourism, and the related infrastructure, is now the main source of income, accounting for around 80 percent of the island's GDP. More than half of all residents work in the sector, and people come from other parts of Spain as well to take up seasonal jobs. Despite its benefits, many locals remain wary of uncontrolled tourism in Mallorca, complaining of spiralling property prices and rents, the dilution of local culture and fears over long-term sustainability. The green-minded government has responded sympathetically, with the introduction of a sustainable tourist tax coming into force on 1 July 2016.

Palau March museum, Palma

TOP TIPS FOR EXPLORING MALLORCA

Menú del día. The lunchtime menu is an economical way to eat as you usually get three hearty courses with bread and a glass of wine or small bottle of water for a low price (usually €10–20).

The rebaixes. Sales in Spain are fantastic, not least because they seem to get longer each year. You'll get the cream of the crop at the start but the real bargains towards the end. Winter sales start on 7 January until 6 March and summer sales last all July and August.

All the island's a stage. Music lovers should head to Mallorca in July or August when the island becomes one long concert, especially in the towns of Deià, Pollença, Valldemossa and Artà, which stage world-class music festivals.

Palma's night of art. With more than 30 participating galleries and museums, Palma's Nit de l'Art gets more ambitious every year. It lasts from 7pm–midnight on the third Thursday in September. Entrance to all exhibitions is free. See www.nitdelartartpalma.com.

The olive oil odyssey. Located several miles outside Sóller, Can Reus Hotel (www.canreushotel.com) in Fornalutx offers gourmet breaks where you can visit a 600-year-old olive farm, harvest your own olives and make your own cold-pressed olive oil.

A quiet beach. The Cala Bòquer is an isolated beach about an hour's walk from Port de Pollença. To get there, head for the roundabout at the top of Carretera For-

mentor, bear left and continue uphill past the Finca Bòquer (a private house) north-east of the town centre to put you on the path of the Bòquer Valley to the beach.

Manacor's pearls. There are few reasons to visit Manacor – the largest town on the east of the island and also where tennis player Raphael Nadal happens to live – other than to invest in Mallorcan pearls. Majorica (Carrer Pere Riche; tel: 971 550 900; www.majorica.com; free) offers guided tours of its facilities and cut-price jewellery.

Take a day trip to Menorca. Catch the morning ferry from Alcúdia and return on the evening one from Ciutadella. Contact Baleària (tel: 902 160 180; www.balearia.net) for details.

Wheelchair-friendly transport. All of Palma's buses have wheelchair access, including those that go to the airport. Several taxi companies have specially adapted taxis: try Mallorca Taxi (www.mallorcataxi.com) or Taxi Tour Mallorca (www.taxitourmallorca.com).

Reduced admission fees. Look out for vouchers in local magazines and newspapers, as well as tourist offices, which give reduced admission fees to attractions.

When it rains. Head inland to Festival Park shopping centre (http://festivalpark.es) in Marratxí (Carretera Palma-Inca Km 7). Here you'll find shops selling discounted clothes from previous seasons, a cinema, a bowling alley, cafés and a children's play area.

Mercat de l'Olivar, Palma

FOOD AND DRINK

It took Spain a long time to realise that its larder was as well stocked and delicious as that of France, its chefs and restaurants every bit as talented. Now it has there's no stopping it, and Mallorca is no exception.

From traditional *cellers* (see page 82) and fishermen's shacks to the proponents of *Nou Cuina Mallorquina* (New Mallorcan Cuisine) – creative young chefs are serving innovative food, and not just in Palma, but all over the island. The sheer diversity of food and eating in Mallorca is thrilling, but you do need to know where to look. The restaurants section of this guide (see page 94) therefore focuses on more local places to eat, and avoids fast food and the bland, 'international-style' meals on offer in the bigger resorts. More importantly, armed with just a little background knowledge of the island's rich culinary heritage you'll be well set up for seeking out hidden gems of your own.

LOCAL CUISINE

Traditional *cuina Mallorquina* (Mallorcan cuisine) reaches its height in the old-fashioned *cellers* of the hinterland, but can be found in many other places, too. Local, humble ingredients – fruit, vegetables, pulses and grains – provide the backbone of the cooking, complemented and enhanced by locally caught fish and seafood (there are plenty of functioning fishing ports, some with excellent restaurants, dotted around the coast, as well as in Palma). Pork – particularly the native *porc negre* – appears in various guises, and island lamb, rabbit and small game birds like partridge and quail are also excellent. Increasingly, small producers of cheese, honey, chocolate and other delicacies are also emerging.

Bread two ways

In nearly every restaurant in Mallorca you will be offered *pa amb oli* (bread and oil), although these days it's ramped up a bit with a small dish of olives and one of *alioli* (garlicky mayonnaise). It's at its best when made with a dark, rustic island bread.

For breakfast you are more likely to be given *pa amb tomaqàet* – the ubiquitous Catalan snack of toasted bread rubbed with a juicy tomato and drizzled with olive oil and a sprinkle of salt. It sounds simple, but is one of the great treasures of the Catalan kitchen and not to be missed. Many hotels serve it as part of their breakfast buffet, while tapas bars do theirs topped with charcuterie, plump little

A wide range of hams to choose from

anchovies or *escalivada* (a salad of roasted vegetables).

The importance of pork

For centuries, pork has been the cornerstone of the islanders' diet. Every family, no matter how poor, fattened a pig every year and, after the *matança* (slaughter), filled the larder with sausages, chops and lard, which formed the foundation of many dishes, both sweet and savoury.

At its most challenging, pork is presented in the form of *frit Mallorquí*, a platter of fried nasty bits liberally seasoned with fennel and mint. More easily digested, perhaps, are the succulent *sobrasadas* (soft pork sausage flavoured with *pimentón*), *butifarró* (coarse grilling sausages), *blanquet* and *camaiot* (cured pork sausages with varying degrees of fat and blood) that you see hanging from the rafters of restaurants and delicatessens.

Popular pork dishes are *llomb amb col* (pork rolled in cabbage leaves and baked) and *arròs brut* (rice with pork or sometimes chicken). *Lechona asada* (roast suckling pig) is really a Christmas dish, but may be found on menus at other times and has been indicated where relevant throughout the routes sections of this book.

Vegetarian delights

Unlike in much of Spain, vegetarian foodies will do well here. The island has a rich variety of vegetables – among

Food markets

If you're into food, don't miss a trawl around Mallorca's various fresh-product markets (especially if you are self-catering). Aside from the sheer bounty of produce available, it's a great way to rub shoulders with local people. Great buys include olive oil, olives, cheese, charcuterie, jams, honey and seasonal fruit and vegetables.

Tuesday morning: head for Artà, which has a wide range of foodstuffs as well as local crafts – see route 10.

Wednesday morning: Sineu is excellent for a taste of old village life, and is one of the very few that still has a livestock section. If you're following route 12, the afternoon market in Colònia de Sant Jordi is an atmospheric place to end the day and pick up snacks for a casual dinner on the beach.

Thursday morning: Inca's market is the largest on the island, while Lluc (route 6) and Sant Llorenç (route 11) also have markets on this day.

Friday morning: stop by to pick up local wines in Binissalem (route 14) as well as tapas items to go with them.

Saturday morning: Palma has three permanent markets, but the farmers'-cum-artisan market that comes into town on Saturday is second to none.

Sunday morning: gather supplies for route 13 in Felanitx, or for route 6 in Valldemossa, and find somewhere to have lunch with a view.

Tumbet – aubergine, potato and red peppers

them aubergines, peppers, chard, crunchy lettuces, good potatoes and juicy tomatoes (including the revered *tomàtiga de Ramellet*, a vine tomato with a thick skin grown specifically for making *pa amb tomàquet*, and which you see hanging on strings in markets all over the island).

In summer, dishes such as *trempó*, a salad of tomatoes, onion and green peppers; are popular; *tumbet*, aubergines, potatoes and sweet red peppers covered in tomato sauce and beaten egg and oven-baked, is a great favourite, as are *aubergines farcides*, aubergines filled with minced meat and tomato sauce (not strictly vegetarian, that one).

Soups

Sopas mallorquinas – invariably referred to in this plural form – are ubiquitous. They are soups made of seasonal vegetables and poured over *pa pagès* (country bread sliced very thin). An interesting variety is the *sopes de matances*, which include small pieces of pork and *setas* (a type of mushroom).

Fish and seafood

Although there are as many fish dishes as there are varieties of fish, two that are especially worth trying are the *anfós al forn* (baked sea bass) and the *caldereta de peix* (spiced fish stew, a version of bouillabaisse). *Caldereta de llagosta*, a rich lobster and tomato stew laced with saffron that is a Menorcan speciality, is also popular, particularly along the north coast. Look out also for *pescado al sal* – whole fish baked in a thick shell of sea salt to preserve the flavour and juices – which, surprisingly, doesn't make the fish taste too salty. Finally, if you're a seafood-lover, don't miss the sweet, pink prawns from Sóller – wildly expensive but absolutely worth it.

Cakes and pastries

Savoury pastries are found in bakeries *(panaderías)* or pastry shops *(pastelerías)*. *Empanades* are small round pies filled with meat and peas; *coca de verdura* is similar to a pizza but is rectangular in shape and eaten cold; while the *cocarois* is half-moon-shaped and filled with *bledes* (chard).

Dolç (desserts) range from the typical *gelat de ametla* served with *coca de gató* (almond ice cream with almond cake) to large, star-shaped biscuits called *crespells* and *coca de patata* (a sweet bread that is a speciality of Valldemossa), as well as *greixonera de brossat*, a type of cheesecake. The *ensaimada*, a spiral-shaped, sugar-dusted confection, is most commonly eaten with coffee at breakfast time.

WHERE TO EAT

At breakfast time you might stop at a pavement café for a cup of coffee and a pastry, then pop into a tapas bar or market stall mid-morning for a quick

Forn des Teatre is a Palma bakery that specialises in ensaimadas

pick-me-up (a glass of cava or vermut, perhaps) and a tapa. For lunch Spanish workers head to a neighbourhood restaurant for a *menú del día* (an inexpensive set meal), then maybe have another tapa somewhere in the early evening. Dinner can be formal or consist of a *tapeo* (a tapas hop) around several bars. Naturally, the best fish restaurants are on the coast and around port areas, while the best fine dining is scattered across the island. And don't discount restaurants in the centre, which showcase some of the finest traditional cooking.

Restaurants in Mallorca cover a wide spectrum, from the excellent to the mediocre, from the local to the international. There has also been a recent emphasis on Basque cooking, which is regarded as one of the best regional cuisines in Spain; and there are refined dishes with a French flair in the more expensive restaurants. Several top-notch chefs are working on the island and, while a meal in one of their restaurants is not cheap, it is considerably less expensive than it would be in one of the European capitals.

DRINKS

Mallorca's wine industry goes from strength to strength, and you won't go far wrong if you stick to locally produced wines (see route 14, page 80). Cava (sparkling wine from Catalunya) is also popular, as is a *caña* (a small draught beer). Most of the beer hails from mainland Spain: San Miguel, Moritz and Estrella de Galica are all good brands to try. Neighbouring Ibiza's Isleña is a light, refreshing pilsner-style beer available all over the island.

PRACTICALITIES

As in the rest of Spain, people in Mallorca eat late. Lunch is generally from 1.30pm to 3.30pm and dinner from around 9pm until late. Restaurants that open their doors earlier tend to be at the touristy end of the spectrum, but this can be useful if you're travelling with children.

Tipping
Tipping is a bit of a grey area. If you want to round up to the nearest euro at the bar if you've only had a snack, that's fine, but not expected. Leaving 5 percent at lunch or dinner is acceptable, and if you are eating somewhere high end, leaving 10 percent is the honourable thing to do.

Food and Drink Prices

Throughout this book, price for a two-course meal for one with a glass of house wine:
€€€€ = over €40
€€€ = €25–€40
€€ = €15–€25
€ = below €15

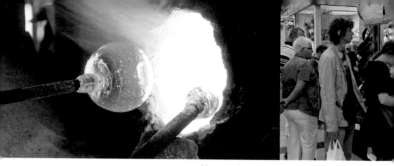

Glassware being blown

SHOPPING

It may not be Madrid or Barcelona, but Mallorca does have a few treats for the consummate shopaholic. Eschew designer labels in favour of island arts and crafts or gourmet products and you'll find a treasure trove of purchases to be discovered.

If Palma is a hotspot for local fashion, interiors and shoes (many of the brands cheaper than they would be on the mainland), the rest of the island has fostered a high-class cottage industry of locally made goods. The discerning traveller can pick up beautiful textiles to translate into bed and table linen back home, classy handmade espadrilles (the rope-soled summer shoe traditional to Spain as a whole), some of the world's finest olive oil and almonds, and a host of other quirky trinkets for gifts.

Most small shops open from 10am–2pm and 5–8pm from Monday to Saturday while high-street chains generally stay open all day, sometimes until 10pm.

WHAT TO BUY

Glass, pottery and ceramics
There are two glass-blowing factories that can be visited: Lafiore (www.lafiore.com), at S'Esgleieta 7km (4 miles) from Valldemossa (see route 6, page 46), and Vidriera Gordiola (www.gordiola.com), just before Algaida on the Palma–Manacor road. Both do a strong line in wacky, psychedelic-coloured bowls and glasses.

The village of Prtol, a short distance northeast of Palma, has the most working kilns on the island. It is also the birthplace of *siurells*, the red, white and green clay-figure whistles, said to have originated in Muslim times. Alternatively, shop for cooking pots: here are two main types: *ollas* (round) and *greixeras* (flat and shallow).

Textiles
The *roba de llengües* (cloth of tongues, pronounced 'yengos'), is named for the colourful, tongue-shaped patterns stamped onto a cotton-linen weave. It's extremely popular for home textiles – tablecloths and bed linen as well as upholstery – and can look surprisingly chic and contemporary. Working looms clatter away at the Museu Martí Vicenç in Pollença (see route 8), but there's a greater selection to buy at Bujosa Textiles, Carrer Bernardo Santa Eugenia 53, Santa Maria del Camí (see route 14).

Leather and straw
Mallorca used to be renowned for the quality of its leather goods, but the industry has declined considerably. Inca is still home to the better-known brands

Mercat de l'Olivar   *Ceramics are a popular purchase*

and factory outlets. If you like shoes, then you'll love shopping in Mallorca. You can go to the factory shop of the quirky shoe company Camper (on the main road around Inca), whose highly individual shoes have become well known. The brand also has outlets in Palma, in Avinguda Jaume III and Carrer Sant Miquel. Elsewhere you will find *abarcas*, the slipper-like sandals from Menorca that have been worn by peasants for centuries and now come in a range of colours for around €25–35. They've become something of a cult item in recent years, the hipster alternative to the espadrille.

In Palma, La Central Mimbrera (www. centralmimbrera.com) makes straw baskets, chairs and other furniture; Alpargateria Llinás, Carrer Sant Miquel 43, sells traditional espadrilles and funky straw shopping bags.

Food and drink

Ensaimadas (see page 18) are sold in individual or family sizes, in appropriate packages for export. Buy them in just about any bakery in Palma or in the departure lounge at the airport. Markets are the best places for olives, cheese and charcuterie, or go to an old-fashioned deli like little Colmado Santo Domingo (see route 3). Vineyards are found around Binissalem–Consell–Santa Maria (see route 14), and in the southeast around Felanitx, and wines are worth buying here. Mallorca is also known for its herbal liqueurs, the most popular being the aperitif Palo Tunel, made in Bunyola.

ANTIQUES AND FLEA MARKETS

There are various well-known antiques shops, most notably in Santa María, Pollença and Sóller. In Palma, Antigüedades Casa Delmonte (http://casa delmonte.es), Persepolis (www.perse polis-antiques.com), and Midge Dalton at Plaça Mercat 20, are good but expensive, while the Baratillo (flea market), which takes over the Avinguda Gabriel Alomari Villalonga every Saturday morning, is great for bargains. Go early.

PALMA'S STORES

Avinguda Jaime III is lined with designer and high-street stores selling fashions, jewellery and gifts. El Corte Inglés, Spain's biggest department store chain, is a good one-stop shop for national and international brands. The Passeig del Born has an interesting variety of shops, ranging from high-quality leather luggage and accessories at Loewe to the city's flagship Zara.

Fine Books, a treasure trove of second-hand English books, is at Carrer Morey 7, near Plaça Major, and there are a number of chic fashion boutiques on Carrer Verí. The Centro Porto Pi, a couple of kilometres west of the centre, is the place to go for high-street brands. Another large shopping complex, FAN Mallorca, opened near Palma in 2016 (Calle Cardenal Rossell s/n).

Folk dancing and music

ENTERTAINMENT

Mallorca is as lively and highly cultured as one could hope for in a place of its size. The great Catalan artist Santiago Rusiñol said islanders 'take the moon' as others 'take the sun', so come prepared to spend long, balmy nights beneath the stars.

The most popular of all Spanish pastimes is to sit out on a plaza in the cool of the night, sipping cold *cañas* (small draught beers) and chatting the night away. Even the smallest of villages seem to burst into life the minute the sun goes down, but Mallorquíns, like all Catalans, are also great patrons of the arts, and Palma is blessed in having a city council that throws considerable funds at keeping her citizens happy. Note that much of the performance art is in Catalan or Spanish, which makes it tough going for non-speakers; though there's plenty else to enjoy that doesn't depend on knowing the language.

THEATRE AND FILM

Theatrical performances and classical concerts usually start at 10pm, and can be found at the fabulously renovated Teatro Principal (www.teatreprincipal.com) and the Teatro Municipal (theatrical performances, of course, will be in Spanish or Catalan), and the Auditorium (www.auditoriumpalma.com) – home to the Ciutat de Palma Symphony Orchestra. There is one original-language cinema – Cine Ciutat, Carrer Emperatrix Eugenia 6 – which regularly shows English-language films.

DANCE

Classical or contemporary dance performances are few and far between, but there are a couple of decent salsa and samba bars, including Made in Brasil, which also offers dance classes. Flamenco isn't big in Mallorca as it has little to do with the island culture, but you can catch performances at Es Foguero (www.esfoguero.com) at Carretera S'Aranjassa Km 10.

MUSIC

Music thrives in Palma, ranging from classical guitar competitions and jazz festivals to piano recitals. There is also a strong jazz and blues scene in the small bars of the old city. Free outdoor concerts – jazz, rock and classical – are held in the beautiful setting of the Parc de la Mar (route 1, see page 30) on some summer evenings. A bar serves drinks and snacks, and there's a party atmosphere.

Being able to dine outdoors is part of the Spanish idyll

Summer is the time for music festivals, most held in beautiful historic buildings. The best known one is the Deià International Music Festival (www.dimf.com). Most performances are in the stunning setting of Son Marroig. The Chopin Festival is held in the cloister of La Cartuja in Valldemossa (www.festivalchopin.com); and the Festival de Pollença (www.festivalpollenca.com) attracts international musicians to the lovely cloister of Sant Domingo. There is a summer music festival with performances in Palma's Castell de Bellver and in the Jardins Fundació March in Cala Ratjada (www.fundacionbmarch.es). Sa Pobla hosts an international jazz festival in August (www.sapobla.cat) and Palma stages events in various venues as part of the Jazz Voyeur Festival (www.jazzvoyeurfestival.com).

BARS AND CAFÉS

Bar-hopping is the favoured nocturnal pursuit in Palma, and few things beat kicking back on a terrace with a glass of wine, a beer or *café con hielo* on a balmy summer night. Café Lírico at Avinguda Antoni Maura 6 or La Bóveda nearby at Carrer Boteria 3 fill up around 10pm and stay full until their doors close at 2–3am. If it's cocktails you seek, don't miss Ábaco (see page 104). It's a Palma institution – kitsch, camp, exotic and expensive, and no trip is complete without experiencing it.

NIGHTLIFE

In the large resorts, notably Magaluf, clubs and discos keep going all night, catering mainly to a very young tourist crowd. The scene is less classy (and drug-fuelled) than in Ibiza, and the best way to find out what's happening is to pick up leaflets in bars in Palma and the rest of the island.

In Palma itself the scene is rather more sophisticated, attracting an older, better-heeled crowd who like their dancing after dinner, their cocktails made with premium liquor and to be in bed by 3am. There are some places where you can dance until dawn, such as the legendary Tito's (www.titosmallorca.com) on the Passeig Marítim and super-hip beach clubs like Puro Beach (www.purobeach.com) at Cala Estancia or Virtual Club (www.virtualclub.es) at Illetas, where the beautiful people go.

Remember that wherever you go, the action doesn't really start until around midnight.

DINNER AND SPECTACLE

A phenomenon that arrived a few decades ago is the 'dinner and spectacle' evening, and despite the rather cheesy overtones they are immensely popular. They range from those suitable for children, such as at Pirates in Magaluf, to a rather swankier affair at the Casino in the Centro Porto Pi. Dress is smart-casual, and you will need your passport to get in.

Windsurfing

ACTIVITIES

It's easy to think of Mallorca as a place with a great beach and little else, but the island is blessed with a diverse landscape that makes it perfect for any number of outdoor pursuits and sports activities.

Of all the Balearic Islands, Mallorca's terrain is the most rewarding, ranging from the gently undulating hills across Es Pla (the central plains), which are ideal for cyclists, to ancient stone paths that crisscross the Tramuntana. You can ramble along cliff paths leading down to secluded bays or tee off on some of the world's most stunning golf courses. Highlights are included within the routes sections, but see below for what else is out there.

BEACH-HOPPING

There are some 80-odd beaches on Mallorca, ranging from wild and windswept to idyllic, isolated coves, and everything in between. Beaches around the Bay of Palma are fairly busy, trendy and well catered for in terms of bars, restaurants and beach clubs. West coast beaches are less accessible and shingle rather than sand, but great if you like isolation. The north coast is mainly family-oriented, with a few hidden gems at the northeastern tip. The east coast is largely built up, save for some less-developed strands like that at Canyamel and the south, once you get away from the Bay of Palma, is wild and unspoilt and all the lovelier for it.

Naturists should head to the designated nudist beaches at Es Trenc (the central part), El Mago (signposted from the road to Cap de Cala Figuera, Bay of Palma) and Cala S'Almunia (walkable from Cala Lombards heading south).

CLIMBING

More extreme sports (deep-water soloing for instance) are starting to take off, but climbing has already gained a firm foothold among more adventurous travellers, thanks to the stunning landscape. Much of it is done on already bolted-in limestone surfaces, a lot of which rise up spectacularly from the sea. Nearly all of it is in the northwest Tramuntana. For information, see www.rocksportmallorca.com.

CYCLING

Mallorca has become a massive destination for keen and professional cyclists – Tour de France training is done here, for example – particularly across the central plains. Good roads and varied terrain mean it offers something for everyone. Tour operators like Inntravel (www.inntravel.co.uk) or Mallorca Cycling (www.mallorcacycling.

Hiking in the hills

Snorkelling in crystal clear water

co.uk) are a good way to go, but you could approach it at a luxurious level, for example at Club Pollentia (www.clubpollentia.com), which offers top-notch kits as well as experienced guides and trainers.

GOLF

There are 20 golf courses on Mallorca. Some of the finest, including the prestigious Son Vida, are clustered around the Bay of Palma. You can get discounted green fees through the website www.simplymallorcagolf.com, as well as information on each course. Many hotels offer golf packages, and there's a good range of places to choose from. You can also pay day green fees at most of the courses.

HIKING

The GR-221 (or Stone Wall Way) is the most popular hiking trail on Mallorca and takes you through the entire Tramuntana (about eight days). There are five refuges to stay in en route, and www.conselldemallorca.net has excellent information, including downloadable maps and route planners. For something less strenuous, there are innumerable well-marked trails all over the island, and new and improved paths are opening all the time.

HOT-AIR BALLOONING

The most spectacular and memorable way to see the island, riding high over the plains and mountains and deep blue sea, is not as inaccessible as you might imagine. Flights cost from €195 and include champagne. Check www.balloonflightsspain.com.

WATER SPORTS

The main activities are sailing, windsurfing and scuba-diving. Palma is a good place to charter a sailing boat to go island hopping (www.mallorcanautic.com). The best area for scuba-diving is the west coast, where sheer cliffs and sheltered bays attract the most diverse sea life. West Coast Divers, www.divinginmajorca.com, offer a wide selection of dives. The near-constant winds of the Cap de Ses Salines attract serious windsurfers, but learners are better off on the north coast; check www.windfriends.com. Spain's longest cableski can be found in Alcúdia – see www.mallorcawakepark.com.

Birdwatching

Mallorca is a great place for birdwatching. Migrant birds visit in spring, and some stay throughout the summer. As many as 200 different species have been recorded. The best place to see a wide variety is the Parc Natural S'Albufera on the Bay of Alcúdia. The Parc Natural de Mondragó in the southeast is another good spot, especially for seabirds, and you may spot black vultures as well as other more common birds of prey in the wild Tramuntana region. For details, go to www.mallorcabirdwatching.com.

Ses Païsses, a Bronze Age talayotic settlement near Artà

HISTORY: KEY DATES

*Mallorca has been ruled by Romans and Moors, gained and lost
independence, founded missions in California, and stood up to Napoleon.
Today, it's one of the most affluent islands in the Mediterranean.*

EARLY PERIOD

1300–1000BC	Megalithic Talayotic period.
400BC	Carthaginians colonise the Balearics.
123BC–AD400	The Romans invade and Mallorca is absorbed into the Roman Empire. It is named 'Balearis Major' and towns including Palmaria (Palma) and Pollentia (Alcúdia) are established.
2nd century AD	Christianity established.
707	First Muslim attack.
848	Moorish rule imposed in the Balearics; it lasts for 300 years.
902	Annexation to the Emirate of Córdoba.
1087–1114	Mallorca becomes an independent taifa.
1114	Pisan-Catalans conquer Mallorca; siege of Palma lasts eight months. After sacking the city, the invaders leave.
1115–1203	The Almorávides, a tribe hailing from North Africa, arrive to provide assistance to the Mallorcan Muslims and stay on to occupy the island, which, as a result, experiences a centenary of prosperity.

THE 13TH TO 18TH CENTURIES

1229	King Jaume I of Aragón conquers Mallorca. Work begins on Palma Cathedral.
1276	Death of Jaume I and creation of the independent Kingdom of Mallorca ruled by Jaume II.
1285	Catalunya attempts to recover the Kingdom of Mallorca by force. Later expedition returned by order of the Pope.
1324–44	Reign of Jaume III, bringing economic prosperity.
1344	Troops of Pedro IV of Aragón invade and reincorporate the islands into the Kingdom of Aragón.

Depiction of the 13th-century Conquest of Mallorca

1479	Kingdoms of Castile and Aragón, including Mallorca, united. Economic decline begins.
1700	Felipe de Bourbón ascends to the throne. Beginning of the War of Spanish Succession.
1785	Treaty of Algiers signed, ending piracy while establishing the Mallorcan 'corsairs'.

THE 19TH CENTURY

1808–13	The War of Independence against Napoleonic troops.
1837	First steamship line between Mallorca and mainland.
1879–98	Period of trading prosperity ends with arrival of the phylloxera epidemic and loss of Spain's last colonies.

THE 20TH CENTURY TO THE PRESENT

1936–9	Spanish Civil War. Mallorca is seized by Nationalist forces.
1939–75	The dictatorship of General Franco brings economic hardship in the early years.
1960s	Mallorca's airport is built and subsequent mass tourism brings prosperity, but great environmental damage.
1975	Juan Carlos I becomes king after the death of Franco.
1983	Five years after the Statute of Autonomy, the Balearics become an autonomous province. Mallorquí is made the official language.
1986	Spain joins the European Community (now the EU).
2000s	The government initiates measures to encourage eco-friendly tourism and move the island's image upmarket.
2002	The euro becomes the official currency of Spain.
2013	More than 70,000 people demonstrate in Palma against the new trilingual educational model – reducing the use of Catalan in schools – initiated by the Partido Popular (PP) government.
2015	Left-wing Partido Socialista Obrero Español (PSOE) and coalition Més per Mallorca (Més) form the new regional government headed by Francina Armengol (PSOE). A record 11.6 million international tourists visit the Balearic Islands.
2016	Sustainable Tourism Tax (better known as 'eco tax') is introduced on the Balearic Islands to raise funds for environmental and heritage protection, as well as for investment in sustainable tourism.

BEST ROUTES

HISTORIC PALMA

*This half-day route offers a distilled version of the history of Palma.
Explore the narrow lanes of the medieval Jewish quarter – now also home
to chic boutiques and trendy restaurants – and add drama with a peek at
the fortress-like cathedral, serene Arabic Baths and a king's secret garden.*

DISTANCE: approximately 3km
(2 miles)
TIME: Leisurely half-day
START: Parc del Mar
END: S'Hort del Rei (The King's
Garden)
POINTS TO NOTE: This route is ideal for
first-time visitors to Palma, showcasing
the oldest, prettiest part of the old
city, which is known as Sa Calatrava.
Because the sights along it are open
year-round, it works at any time of year
and could easily connect with all or
some of route 2, if you wanted to cram
a lot into a day.

Set around a sheltered bay, **Palma** is
a large, cosmopolitan city, with around
400,500 inhabitants – almost half the
permanent population of Mallorca. It is
very much a Mediterranean city, with
palm trees and bushes of fragrant ole-
ander, outdoor cafés with colourful
awnings, and yachts bobbing in the bay
among working vessels. It's smart and
urbane, with designer boutiques, smart

restaurants and chic art galleries hidden in narrow alleys.

The city also has a colourful cultural
history. Founded by the Romans in
123BC as Palmeria, it was a fairly unim-
portant backwater until the arrival of the
Moors in AD902. Seeing the city's potential, they built mosques (one where the
cathedral now stands), bathhouses and
other tokens of civilised life.

This tour starts where the 21st century and the Middle Ages meet, at the
Parc del Mar.

PARC DEL MAR

Start your walk at the entrance to the
Moorish Walls at the western end of
the **Parc del Mar ❶**, which gives the
most commanding view. The contemporary concrete and wood landscaping
provides a striking contrast to the old
city and the sea beyond. In the middle
is an artificial lake designed to reflect
Palma's imposing cathedral, an essential stop for photography enthusiasts.
It is also home to a number of modern
sculptures, including a vibrant mural by

Parc del Mar

Joan Miró. Head west along the Passeig Marítim for breakfast or a coffee at **Cappuccino Grand Café**, see ❶ before you start.

Follow the walls around to the east and you will eventually reach a plain arch – the **Porta de la Portella** ❷ – the official doorway to the Casc Antic (Old City) under Arabic rule and the heart of the Call (Jewish quarter) during the 13th and 14th centuries. Straight ahead at Carrer de la Portella 5 is the **Museu de Mallorca** ❸ (http://museudemallorca.caib.es; Tue–Fri 10am–6pm, Sat–Sun 11am–2pm; the building is partially closed for restoration). Housed in the resplendent mansion Ca La Gran Cristiana, it is well worth a stop to take a peek at Roman remains, Gothic and Islamic art, and get a sense of the rich history of this comparatively small city.

Palma's Jewish heart

This compact, car-free neighbourhood of narrow cobblestoned streets was home to one of the most prolific and wealthy Jewish communities in the entire Mediterranean in the Middle Ages, although Jews had been here since Roman times. This cultural mix accounts in some part for the diverse architectural styles that make up one of the most handsome cities in the Mediterranean, much of which spun out from a sacred hill in the centre known as **Monte Sión** ❹ – now the site of a church.

One of the great Jewish celebrities of the 14th century was the cartographer Jafuda Cresques, who was credited with drawing up the first Catalan Atlas as well as the maps used by Christopher Columbus. His house still stands on Carrer Botones, due east of the Church of Monte Sión. It is not open to the public, but there is a small monument of Jafuda.

ARABIC BATHS

From the museum, turn right onto Carrer Pureza and immediately right again onto Carrer Serra and you'll find one of the last remaining vestiges of the Moorish occupation. The **Banys Arabs** ❺ (Arabic Baths; Carrer Serra 7; daily Apr–Nov 9.30am–7pm, Dec–Mar until 5.30pm), which once housed the hot baths, are well preserved, with a pristine cupola pinpricked with tiny skylights. The secret, shaded gardens also provide a superb retreat if you're looking for somewhere to escape with a book for an hour or two.

CATHOLIC CHURCHES

Head north along Carrer de Santa Clara, then right onto Carrer Pont y Vich and Carrer Pau Nadal and you'll pop out on pretty Plaça Sant Francesc, where there is a small chapel of the same name. The **Basílica de San Francisco** ❻ is something of a hidden treasure, notable for having one of the most beautiful cloisters in Spain, with delicately carved

Ajuntament (City Hall)

columns and arches. It is also the final resting place of Ramon Llull (1235–1315), who was credited with penning the first great literary work in Catalan.

Palmas's oldest café

A couple of streets away heading north, the beautifully tiled 18th-century **Can Joan de S'Aigo**, see ②, on Carrer de Can Sanç 10, was the artist Joan Miró's favourite café, and there is no better place for a quick pick-me-up.

PALMA'S PARLIAMENT

Wiggle your way westwards over onto Carrer Colóm, then head south to the **Ajuntament** ❼ (City Hall; www.palma. cat; fortnightly tours in English (Sun at noon), booking essential, tel: 618 914 517) with a striking overhanging roof, supported by carved beams. Enter the street-level hallway and you will get to see a couple of ceremonial Mallorcan *gigantes* (giants) built of papier-mâché and hauled out for every local celebration. Further down the street, the magnificent ochre colonnades of the **Parlament de les Illes Baleares** ❽ have been the hub of city politics since the 13th century.

A hard left along the Carrer de l'Almudaina brings you to another of the city's original Arabic gates, the **Arc de l'Almudaina** ❾, which some experts suggest could date back to Roman times. If you're hungry, the excellent **Las Olas** bistro, see ❸, is just up the road on Car-

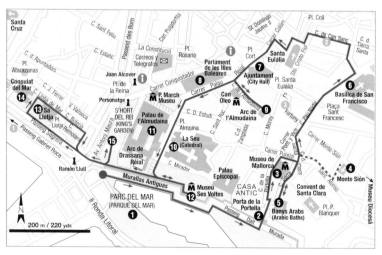

La Seu cathedral *Detail of Basílica de San Francisco*

rer Fortuny and is a great choice for a casual lunch.

CATHEDRAL BY THE SEA

Head back down Carrer Palau Reial and the city's crowning glory, the cathedral known simply as **La Seu ❿** (Carrer Capiscolato 2; www.catedralde mallorca.info; Mon–Fri June–Sept 10am–6.15pm, Apr, May and Oct until 5.15pm, Nov–Mar until 3.15pm, Sat until 2.15pm all year) towers up before you (Seu means a bishop's seat). Like most places of religious significance in Spain, its first stone was laid on the site of a former mosque, in this case by Jaume I in 1229, and it took hundreds of years to complete. It encompasses a range of architectural styles, from the twisted Gothic features of the 16th century right through to Modernista flourishes added by legendary Barcelona architect Antoni Gaudí between 1902 and 1914. Check out his wrought-iron 'crown of thorns' – the baldacchino – over the altar.

The immense sense of space and light here is largely due to seven rose windows, the most spectacular of which has a 12m (40ft) diameter. Externally, its flying buttresses give it a fortress-like appearance, while its watery surroundings make it seem like it's floating out to sea. Take the time to walk around it, for it is truly extraordinary from any angle and at any time of day. The adjacent **museum** (same hours as cathedral) is

worth a look too – it contains, among other curios, Jaume I's self-invented portable altar.

ROYAL PALACES

Next door to the cathedral is the **Palau de l'Almudaina ⓫** (Tue–Sun Apr–Sept 10am–8pm, Oct–Mar until 6pm), also built on the site of a Moorish fortress. It was revamped by Jaume I in Gothic style and since 1985 has been the official residence of the king of Spain when he is in Mallorca. The 14th-century Capella de Santa Ana and 13th-century Sala del Tinell (Throne Room) are the principal highlights, along with some impressive Flemish tapestries. It also has a very pretty courtyard (Patio del Rei).

Palma's coat of arms, as seen at the Palau, features a spread-eagled bat above the shield. Various legends surround its significance, but the most popular is that a bat flew into a drum one night while Christian soldiers lay slumbering. The noise it made woke them up just in time to save themselves from a marauding Moorish army, which contributed to their eventual reconquest of the island.

Shipyards and stock exchange

Head down the steps between the cathedral and the Almudaina, to what was once the royal shipyards. The site is now occupied by the **Museu Ses Voltes ⓬** (times vary according to exhibitions; free), set into the city walls and

Tapestry in Palau de l'Almudaina

Food and Drink

① CAPPUCCINO GRAND CAFÉ

Passeig Marítím 1; tel: 971-282 162; www.grupocappuccino.com; B, L and D; €

This port-side café is one of a small chain with several branches in attractive locations throughout the city. It's a great place for breakfast and a *café con leche* on the sunny terrace before you start your route, and also does good lunches.

② CAN JOAN DE S'AIGO

Carrer de Can Sanç 10; tel: 971 710 759; www.canjoandesaigo.webs-sites.com; B, Br and AT; €

Think regal glamour at this 300-year-old café. Settle into one of the velvet banquettes for hot chocolate and an *ensaimada* (the snail-shaped pastry sprinkled with icing sugar) on chilly days. If it's hot, you can get a scoop of almond ice cream to take away.

③ LAS OLAS

Carrer Fortuny 5; tel: 971 21 49 05; www.lasolasbistro.com; Mon and Tue L, Wed–Sat L and D; €€

A great local bistro that offers an excellent value, three-course *menú del día*. Expect creative Franco-Mediterranean dishes such as watermelon gazpacho and roast *bacalao* (salt cod) with apple *alioli*. Just the ticket after a morning tramping around the sights.

devoted to works by contemporary Mallorcan artists.

From here head back along the walls and cross over Avenida Antoni Maura to the Plaça de Sa Llotja, and you'll come to the whimsical-looking turreted **Sa Llotja** ⓭ (open when exhibitions are on; free), built by Guillem Sagrera in the 15th century as the merchants' stock exchange. Today, this elegant Gothic building is used for art exhibitions, a role for which its beautiful airy interior is well suited. Next door, the 17th-century **Consulat del Mar** ⓮ was built as a maritime court – today used as provincial government offices – and is easily identified by the cannon and a large anchor standing outside it.

A KING'S GARDEN

Retrace your steps along Carrer Marina and Carrer Boteria (parallel to the Passeig Marítím), turning north onto Avenida Antoni Maura to the **S'Hort del Rei** ⓯ (King's Garden), a park filled with pools, fountains and shady greenery, among which stand several arresting modern sculptures, and a bronze *hondero* (the name of the early sling-throwers – in ancient times, Balearic islanders were famed for their skills with a sling in battle).

At the upper end, near Miró's famous sculpture called *Personatge* – popularly known as simply 'The Egg' – is a pleasant little bar with tables and chairs outside, the perfect spot for a nice cold beer at the end of your walk.

Es Baluard Museu d'Art Modern

PALMA'S GALLERIES

Despite its size, Palma has gained a reputation as one of the most important art destinations in Spain. It has several privately owned collections as well as a few world-class galleries to rival those of Madrid and Barcelona.

DISTANCE: 1.5km (1 mile)
TIME: One day or a leisurely half-day
START: Es Baluard
END: Plaça de Espanya
POINTS TO NOTE: This route is great for out-of-season visits when the museums and galleries are quieter. The first two galleries are within easy walking distance of each other, while the Pilar and Joan Miró Foundation is best accessed by bus. You could also connect to route 7 by hopping on the Sóller train at Plaça de Espanya.

Over the last hundred years Mallorca has become increasingly prosperous, a fact highlighted by its love of art. There are large galleries, outdoor sculpture parks and private collections stashed in stately homes all over the island. This route covers Palma's big three.

ES BALUARD

The jewel in Palma's artistic crown is located in a former military stronghold, built in the early 16th century to protect the town against marauders. In 1952 it passed into private hands, and after a lengthy period of stagnation it was slated for destruction. A horrified public stepped in and eventually it was given to Palma City Council, who decided to turn it into a modern art museum, **Es Baluard Museu d'Art Modern ❶** (Plaça Porta de Santa Catalina 10; www.esbaluard.org; Tue–Sat 10am–8pm,Sun until 3pm), which opened in 2004.

A local architect's firm, On Diseño, was commissioned to integrate the ancient walls with a more modern design, and the result is a stunning contemporary gallery showcasing rotating exhibitions, that attracts big names from all over the world. It's worth setting aside a couple of hours just to appreciate the space fully.

The original sandstone walls of the fortress soften the effects of the steel and concrete, giving it an unexpectedly organic feel. Spacious and light-filled, it seamlessly combines interior and exterior spaces, encouraging visitors to interact with the building as well as the art within it. A walkway that wraps

Exhibits in the Fundació Juan March

around the roof affords spellbinding views of the sea and city.

The 'Aljub'

The main exhibition space for concerts and installations occupies the former 'Aljub', a Moorish name for a freshwater reservoir. Until the mid-20th century it supplied fresh water to the entire Sant Pere district, channelled from the La Vila spring in Esporles along what is now Bonaire Street. Should you start to fade, the rooftop café and terrace offer sweeping views of the port.

MUSEU FUNDACIÓN JUAN MARCH

From Es Baluard it takes just 15 minutes to walk northeast across the old city to the splendid **Museu Fundació Juan March** ❷ (Sant Miquel 11; www.march.es; Mon–Fri 10am–6.30pm, Sat 10.30am–2pm; free). Weave up Carrer Olivera, through Plaça Santa Cruz and along Carrer Paz to Plaça Rei Joan Carles, then turn right along La Unió to the arcaded Plaça Major and north onto Carrer Sant Miquel, a pretty and highly enjoyable walk, which will land you in the 17th-century mansion Can Gallard des Canyar, now home to an impressive selection of the March family's extensive private art collection.

The March legacy

Juan March made his fortune in banking in the late 1930s, when he became known as 'Franco's Banker' after funding his right-wing nationalist party. His

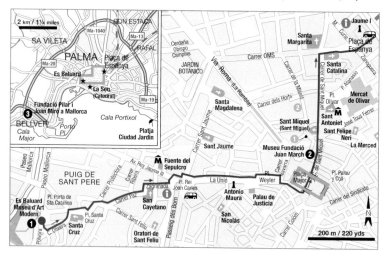

A lecture in Es Baluard   *Canvasses at the Fundació Pilar i Joan Miró*

extreme Conservatism clearly paid off, because by 1955 he was seventh-richest man in the world, and his legacy lives on not only in the form of the bank which is still family owned, but in various cultural guises around the island.

Home of the Spanish vanguard

What is most striking about the collection is the sheer range. Dark expressionism by Miquel Barceló stands shoulder to shoulder with metal sculptures by Eduardo Chillida; surrealist and technical paintings by Salvador Dalí alongside big bolts of primary colour by Antoni Tàpies. These are just a few of the big names. There is also a permanent space dedicated solely to Picasso's etchings. Allow an hour or so to absorb it fully, then treat yourself to a snack at **L'Antiquari**, see ❶, or a more substantial lunch at **Marc Fosh Resturant**, see ❷.

PLAÇA DE ESPANYA

To continue to the **Fundació Pilar i Joan Miró a Mallorca ❸**, head for the Plaça de Espanya straight up Carrer de Sant Miquel. Turn right at Plaça Porta Pintada, which pops you out on Plaça de Espanya.

Miró Foundation

Bus numbers 3 or 46 take you straight from the Plaça de Espanya to the Fundació Pilar i Joan Miró a Mallorca (Carrer Saridakis 29; www.fpjmiro.org; Tue–Sat mid-May–mid-Sept 10am–7pm, Sun 10am–3pm, mid-Sept–mid-May 10am–6pm, Sun 10am–3pm; free on Sat) in about 30 minutes. It is a gleaming white building designed by Rafel Moneo, and the light in the gardens is at its most beautiful after lunchtime.

The prolific collection totals 118 paintings, 275 mixed media pieces, 1,512 drawings and 35 sculptures, covering the period of 1908–81. It also includes his personal collection of works by other artists and sculptors, newspaper and magazine clippings and other tokens of inspiration.

Food and Drink

❶ L'ANTIQUARI

Carrer Arabí 5; tel: 871 572 313; L and D; €
Hip retro café noted for its quiches, ham and cheese platters and toasted sandwiches. It's also a great place for a drink in the evening and there are regular live music concerts.

❷ MARC FOSH RESTAURANT

Carrer de la Missió, 7A; tel: 971 720 114; www.marcfosh.com; L and D, closed Sun; €€€–€€€€
Acclaimed chef Marc Fosh's latest venture is a Michelin-starred restaurant offering a three-course lunch menu using fresh ingredients and an inspired à la carte menu with dishes like venison with pumpkin and sea bream with olive oil parmentier, raisins, spinach and pine nuts.

Fresh vegetables for sale

PALMA FOR FOODIES

Mallorca is establishing itself as one of the hottest food destinations in Europe, with Palma at the head of the table. This route wiggles through the centre from the Santa Catalina market to a well-stocked cheese shop.

DISTANCE: 2.5km (1.5 miles)
TIME: Half-day
START: Mercat de Santa Catalina
END: Sa Formatgeria
POINTS TO NOTE: Do this route in the morning when market produce is at its freshest and you can work up a healthy appetite for lunch (on Sunday the featured places are shut). You could split it in two and do your shopping in the morning, before linking up with routes 1 or 2.

There is something thrilling about shopping for food in a foreign place, and Palma is no exception.

MERCAT DE SANTA CATALINA

The **Mercat de Santa Catalina** ❶ (Plaça Navegació; www.mercatdesantacatalina. com; Mon–Sat 7am–5pm) occupies an entire block of the Santa Catalina neighbourhood. Rub shoulders with local people, learn about the fish and seafood and see what fruit and vegetables are in season. Shop for cheese and sausages and olive oils at the richly laden Charcuterie Selecta Izquierdo stall (www.charcuteri-aizquierdo.com); for *pimentón* and saffron, marcona almonds and pine nuts, go to Especias Crespi (www.especiascrespi. com). To get really into the spirit of things, have a tapa and a mid-morning glass of wine at the bar near Carrer de Soler exit. For something more substantial, the bars and restaurants that surround the market serve solid, unpretentious food, see ❶.

SPECIALIST SHOPS

Cross back into the centre of the old town for the best of the rest. The most direct route is along the La Llotja section of the old walls (see route 1), left onto Avenida Antoni Maura and Carrer Conquistator, and left again onto Carrer Santo Domingo. Right at its head you'll find the **Colmado Santo Domingo** ❷ (www.colmadosanto domingo.com; Mon–Fri 10.15am–7.30pm, Sat until 7pm), one of the city's oldest shops and purveyors of the finest *porc negre* artisan sausage in town.

Minutes away, **La Pajarita** ❸ (Carrer Sant Nicolau 2–4, www.lapajarita1872.

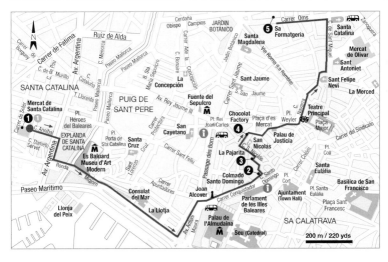

Find classic Mallorcan sweet treats at La Pajarita

com; Mon 10am–2pm, 4.30–8pm, Tue–Fri 10am–8pm, Sat until 2pm) is an old-fashioned sweet and cake shop and the place to pick up a giant *ensaimada* packed into a cardboard box and tied up with string. The interior is a delight, with crystal chandeliers, Modernista tiles and a counter piled high with jewel-coloured sweet treats.

Continue along Carrer San Nicolás, turning right onto Carrer Mercado where the **Chocolat Factory** ❹ (Plaça d'es Mercat 9; www.chocolatfactory.com; Mon–Sat 10.30am–9pm) has an extraordinary range of products, ranging from truffles and bonbons to gourmet, single-estate chocolate and children's snacks.

From here it's a leisurely stroll northeast to Carrer del Oms and **Sa Formatgeria** at No. 30 ❺ (www.saformatgeria.com; Mon–Sat 9am–9pm), which sells a wide variety of cheeses including several from Mallorca such as Ruat organic goat's cheese. They also stock wine, olive oil and other regional products from the Balearics.

Food and Drink

❶ EL PERRITO

Carrer Aníbal 20; tel: 971 455 916; B, Br and L, Drinks; €€

Popular for post-shopping coffee, brunch and laid-back lunches at the weekend, this place positively bristles with atmosphere. Try to nab a seat out on the pavement terrace where you can watch the world go by.

Port Adriano

ANDRATX TO BANYALBUFAR

The southwest is a curious mix, where mass tourism meets the glitzy jet set then leads on to sleepy villages, terraced hillsides and glorious clifftop views. The route can be crammed into a day, but it is best to stay overnight.

DISTANCE: 33km (21 miles)
TIME: 1–2 days
START: Port Adriano
END: Banyalbufar
POINTS TO NOTE: This route should be travelled by car, but includes a possible boat trip and two hikes. It's best done in the summer if you want to make the boat trip to Sa Dragonera and swim in the sea, while spring and autumn are preferable for hiking. If you do plan to include either of the hikes featured, note they are fairly strenuous and not suitable for small children.

This route takes you from the swish port of Port Adriano to sleepy Sant Elm, then via a coast road with jaw-dropping views to a ruined monastery and the terraced hillsides of Banyalbufar, where there are some excellent restaurants.

PORT ADRIANO

To get to **Port Adriano** ❶ (Santa Ponça s/n; www.portadriano.com), drive west along the main highway, the Ma-1, from Palma for around 10km (6 miles). Turn left for Santa Ponça and it is well sign-posted from there. Built in 1992, Port Adriano was handed over to French designer Philippe Starck in 2007 to be remodelled as the Balearic power port for super yachts, complete with a heli-port and luxury shops and restaurants. Visitors can enjoy its unique Starck design while strolling the docks, admiring the pleasure palaces of the rich and famous. There are plenty of places to grab a cup of coffee before continuing.

ADRIANO TO ANDRATX

The Ma-1 continues northwards to **Andratx** ❷, which is spread messily out beneath the twin peaks of the S'Esclop mountain (926m/3,038ft). The town sits at the heart of a fertile agricultural region and is refreshingly low-key in terms of tourism. Originally founded as a refuge for Christian settlers, it was the home of both the bishop of Barcelona and King Jaume I in the 13th century, and at

Andratx   *Sant Elm*

the top of the town, above the Plaça del Pou, the towering walls of the fortress-like church of Santa Maria still stand proud and strong. Check out the brilliant Centro Cultural Andratx (Estanyera, 2; www.ccandratx.com; Mar–Oct Tue–Fri 10.30am–7pm, Sat and Sun until 4pm, Nov–Feb Tue–Sat 10.30am–4pm), the largest centre of contemporary art on the island, set in stunning surroundings. There are also artists' workshops, a café and bookshop on site. Other than that, there's not a great deal to see or do here except on Wednesdays, which is market day, but it's a pleasant enough town for a stroll.

S'Arracó's colonial architecture

On the western edge of Andratx is the tiny village of **S'Arracó ❸**. Once said to have taken nine hours by cart to reach from Palma, it is difficult to imagine now, but the village retains its atmosphere and is good place to get a glimpse of the *casas de indianos* (houses built by Mallorcans returning from the colonies), now highly coveted second homes.

PARADISE ISLANDS

Continuing west from S'Arracó you will come to the pretty port town of **Sant Elm ❹** – the gateway to the desert island of **Sa Dragonera ❺**. Once the hideout of Redbeard the pirate, these days it's the favoured haunt of a multitude of Lilford's lizards which enjoy lounging around in the sun. *Margarita* boat tours (€13; tel: 639-617 545/

Watchtower at the Mirador de Ses Ànimes

629-606 614; www.crucerosmarga-rita.com), run back and forth to the island every 30 minutes from 9.45am to 2.15pm between April and September, and 9.45am–12.15pm between February and March and in October. It is a proper paradise for those who make the trip – mainly walkers and birdwatchers who come to see the rare Eleanora's falcon and impressive numbers of seabirds. Scattered around are a number of little islets like Es Pantaleu, Sa Mitjana and Els Cala-fats, all of which are good for bathing and snorkelling. Remember to take a

picnic – if you're going on a Wednes-day, stop off at Andratx's weekly mar-ket to pick up some goodies – or head back to **Arasa**, see ❶, for lunch in Sant Elm as you won't find anywhere to eat on the island.

The Sa Trapa trail

Back in Sant Elm you can walk to the ruins of the ancient **Sa Trapa** ❻ mon-astery without leaving dry land. It is a popular walk and well signposted, but it's not suitable for small children and requires a certain fitness level – expect to take at least four hours to do the round trip. The scenery, particu-larly when the spring flowers are in full bloom, is spectacular, and the views of Sa Dragonera are second to none.

ANDRATX TO ESTELLENCS

Back in Andratx, continue driving north in the direction of Banyalbufar on Ma-1. At around Km 99 you will spot the famed **Mirador de Ricard Roca** ❼, which has jaw-dropping views of the deep-blue Mediterranean, provid-ing you can see past the tour buses. It may be better to bypass the crowds and keep going until you reach **Estel-lencs** ❽ (pronounced 'Es-ta-yencs'). The village is postcard-perfect, with narrow, cobblestoned streets and pretty honey-coloured stone cottages, their window boxes spilling over with geraniums and ferns.

Cliff walk

For keen walkers the most rewarding way to get to Banyalbufar from Estel-lencs is to walk along the cliff paths of the GR-221 (www.gr221.info; Mal-lorca Tramuntana Sud, Editorial Alpina provides detailed maps of the region, priced at around €12). The area around Es Rafal has been closed for more than a decade due to disputes over land ownership (the ruling in favour of pub-lic use of the land has already been announced but is subject to appeal), but there is a well-signposted alterna-tive route. It takes a good day to get there and back, but it's an unforgetta-ble walk with a couple of opportunities to jump into the sea at the start and fin-ish of the trail. A picnic, plenty of water and sunscreen are essential.

Cala Estellencs

If you are spreading this route over two days and have booked accommodation in Estellencs, end your day with a dip at pint-sized **Cala Estellencs** ❾. Take a hard left downhill onto Carrer Eusebi Pascual on entering the village, and follow it down to the sea (about 2km/1.25 miles). The rocky inlet and beach are ringed by tiny boathouses where local fishermen keep their nets and gear, and it's a wonderfully secluded spot for a sunset swim.

ESTELLENCS TO BANYALBUFAR

This section of the drive passes another viewpoint, the **Mirador de Ses Ànimes**, where there are stunning views of the coast from a 16th-century watchtower, the Torre Verger, which was built during the time when Mallorca was regularly being attacked by North Africans; along the route you get plenty of opportunity to admire the ancient Moorish terracing of the steep hillsides of pretty **Banyalbufar** ❿. On the surrounding embankment villagers once cultivated the now-legendary *malvasia* wine. Although the wine is no more, its name lives on in local parlance as a synonym for 'marvellous'.

If you arrive here in time for lunch, **Ca'n Toni Moreno**, see ❷, does great fish right on the beach. And if you arrive closer to sunset, **Hotel Mar-i-Vent**, see ❸, which was a chic, summer retreat for well-heeled Palma residents during the 1940s, is now a good bet for drinks or dinner.

Food and Drink

❶ ARASA

Avinguda Jaime I 6, Sant Elm; tel: 971 239 272; L and D; €€

This simple seaside restaurant serves some of the freshest fish and seafood in the area and is great for tapas and salads. The terrace gives views straight over to Sa Dragonera, and it's a great place to kick back and do nothing for a couple of hours.

❷ CA'N TONI MORENO

Carrer des Port d'es Canonge 2, Banyalbufar; tel: 971 610 426; L and D; €€€

A short detour from Banyalbufar is this pretty shingle beach with one lone, inauspicious-looking restaurant. The fish is first rate, particularly the *caldereta de langosta* (a local lobster stew enriched with tomatoes and saffron).

❸ HOTEL MAR I VENT

Carrer Major 49, Banyalbufar; tel: 971 618 000; www.hotelmarivent.com; L and D; €€

It's worth calling ahead to bag a spot on the spectacular terrace, which occupies a beautiful position on the edge of the cliff. The food here is simple Mallorquín fare for the most part, with Sunday lunch paella the star of the show.

Bunyola's distinctive green shutters

VILLAGES OF THE TRAMUNTANA

This beautiful, but relatively unknown region takes in some of the most spectacular vistas and prettiest villages of the Serra de Tramuntana.

DISTANCE: 37km (23 miles)
TIME: 1 day
START: Bunyola
END: Lloseta
POINTS TO NOTE: The villages are linked by the Ma-2110, which makes the route easy to follow, but the road is full of hairpin bends, so it's slow going. If you don't have time for the whole route, or don't want to rent a car, take the Sóller train from Palma to Bunyola (www.trende soller.com), which links to route 7.

The pretty villages of Bunyola, Orient, Alaró and Lloseta can all be used as bases for a variety of well-marked hiking trails. If you want to spend a couple of days exploring the area, Orient, with good restaurants and hotels, is the best option.

BUNYOLA

Driving into **Bunyola** ❶ on the Ma-11 from Palma, you soon notice the striking yellow-tiled spire and bright green shutters of the Modernista Villa Francisca, which gives a sense of the bourgeois nature of

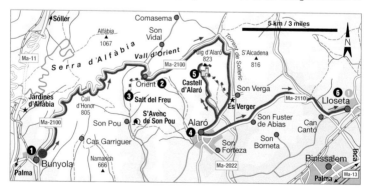

Castell d'Alaró

these mountain villages. In the 19th century it was known for its wine (the name is from the Arabic word for vineyard) and was quickly adopted by the upper classes of the time as an escape from the city.

Associations with an exclusive clientele continue – in 2015 Sir Richard Branson added a beautiful Mallorcan retreat, Son Bunyola, to his portfolio. Yet while the village is popular with second-home owners, it has largely escaped the ravages of tourism. Bunyola is a sweet place for a cup of coffee, especially on Saturday mornings when the market takes over the main plaza. For walkers, the wooded glades that surround the town make for some good rambling. Paths are signposted from the train station, but if it's serious hiking you're after, continue on to Orient.

ORIENT

Leave Bunyola on the Ma-2100 with the majestic Serra d'Alfàbia rising up to your left. Once over the pass, the descent into the lush green fields of the Vall d'Orient is breathtaking, and the small village of **Orient ❷**, is no less lovely.

The highlight is the mysterious trail to the **Salt del Freu ❸** – a 25m (82ft) high waterfall and misty river that runs through a forest of ancient oaks.

ALARÓ

Continuing towards **Alaró ❹**, the road runs between two tabletop mountains: S'Alcadena to the left and the Puig d'Alaró to the right, with the ruins of the **Castell d'Alaró ❺** (www.castellalaro.cat) perched on top, offering dormitory accommodation and a restaurant with homemade cakes. One of three such structures on the island, the castle is famous for resisting for four years the Aragonese invasion of 1285, and for the grisly fate of the two commanders in charge after they capitulated.

The walk from the town of Alaró (3 hours each way) to the castle is one of the most popular on the island and well signposted. You can't drive all the way to it, but if you're looking for an easier hike, turn off at Km 18 and park at the **Es Verger** restaurant. It takes about an hour each way from there.

LLOSETA

Lloseta ❻ is a pleasant spot to end the tour, with just enough interest for a stroll and a look around the shops. Don't miss lunch at **Santi Taura**, see ❶, one of the most exciting restaurants on the island.

Food and Drink

❶ SANTI TAURA

Carrer Joan Carles 1, Lloseta; tel: 656 738 214; www.restaurantsantitaura.com; L and D, closed Tue, Sun D and Mon L; €€€
A star of new Mallorcan cuisine, this elegant little place serves just one tasting menu, an excellent-value, six-course extravaganza of locally sourced, seasonal dishes. The menu changes every Wednesday. Booking essential.

Valldemossa

VALLDEMOSSA TO LLUC

The central Tramuntana has long attracted artists, writers and musicians. This tour delves into their lives: from Frédéric Chopin and George Sand's cell in the monastery at Valldemossa and Robert Graves's writer's hideaway on the cliffs of Deià, to Mallorca's most illustrious scholar, Ramon Llull.

DISTANCE: 54km (33 miles)
TIME: 1 day
START: Valldemossa
END: Lluc
POINTS TO NOTE: This stretch of coast is far from undiscovered these days – come high season the tour buses and rental cars can be bumper to bumper. To avoid the crush, come in early spring or late autumn, or midweek rather than at the weekend. There are numerous places to eat en route, as well as a handful of places to stay, ranging from the luxurious to inexpensive pensions and basic rooms at the Lluc monastery.

Individual experiences can be so different. Sand's winter in the monastery in Valldemossa in 1838 was so miserable she was compelled to vent her unhappiness in a book entitled *A Winter in Mallorca*. Robert Graves had far happier experiences, pitching up in neighbouring Deià in 1929, where he stayed for the rest of his life. Indeed it is largely thanks to Graves that the little village became such a magnet for writers, artists and celebrities.

VALLEDEMOSSA

The truth is, **Valldemossa** ❶ isn't as charming as it once was. Though still pretty enough, hordes of day-trippers from Palma have turned it into something of a theme park, albeit a fairly classy one. The main draw is the Carthusian monastery, **La Reial Cartoixa** Ⓐ (www.cartujadevalldemossa.com; Apr–Sept Mon–Sat 9.30am–7pm, Mar and Oct until 6pm, Feb and Nov until 5.30pm, Dec and Jan until 3.30pm, Sun Feb–Nov 10am–1pm), where Frédéric Chopin and George Sand occupied two of the cells after the monks had been expelled in 1835. At least that is what was believed until a story broke in 2010 speculating that the cells purporting to be theirs were not, and the piano played during today's Chopin-themed concerts wasn't his either. What is certain is that Chopin and Sand stayed and worked somewhere within the confines of the monastery, and

La Reial Cartoixa   *Deià*

the Chopin concerts are worth attending regardless of whose piano it is.

Apart from said cells, there is an atmospheric pharmacy stocked with beautiful 18th-century ceramic jars, great views from the monks' gardens, and the neighbouring **Palau de Rei Sanxo** Ⓑ and municipal museum (closes 15 minutes later than the monastery). The latter has a small but excellent modern art collection, including works by Francis Bacon and Max Ernst.

It won't take you long to get around either of these, so stroll through the narrow, smooth-stoned streets around flower-decked **Plaça de Santa Catalina Tomàs** Ⓒ. The square is named after Mallorca's very own saint, who was born here in 1531; there are two shrines to her in the town, and nearly every house has a tiled picture of her on the wall. Stop for a coffee and the local speciality, *coca de patata* (sugar-dusted potato buns) in **Plaça Ramón Llull** Ⓓ before heading on your way.

VALLDEMOSSA TO DEIÀ

Leave town on the Avinguda Arxi duc Lluís Salvador in the direction of Sóller. When you get to the end of an avenue of plane trees the road curves sharply left for Deià, and with the first right you can head to the dinky Port de Valldemossa, a steep drive full of switchbacks and hairpin bends. The coastal Ma-10 is breathtaking, offering endless sea views to the left, and groves of ancient,

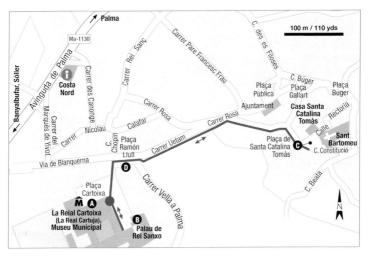

Sunset from Son Marroig

gnarled olive trees among huge boulders to the right.

Son Marroig

En route to Deià you will pass **Son Marroig** ❷ (www.sonmarroig.com; Mon–Sat Apr–Sept 9.30am–7pm, Oct–Mar 10am–6pm), one of the island's great stately homes (*possessió*). It was once owned by Archduke Ludwig Salvator of Habsburg-Lorraine and Bourbon, who installed in the garden a small marble temple from which to gaze on the rock of Na Foradada, carved by nature with a keyhole-shaped window.

The **Sa Foradada**, see ❶, nearby is a good lunch stop, with great views and tasty homemade food.

The Graves legacy

Deià ❸ is set against the steep, rocky slopes of Puig Es Teix and is relatively lively for its size. There is little of note in the pretty, golden-stone village save for the Església de Sant Joan Bautista and its cemetery, the final resting place of Mallorca's most famous adopted son. The small flat stone says simply: 'Robert Graves, Poeta, 1895–1985'.

Graves acted as a magnet for would-be painters and writers (as well as established writers such as Anaïs Nin and the young

Gabriel García Márquez, and Hollywood stars like Ava Gardner). Long after he died, the glitterati kept coming. Michael Douglas and Catherine Zeta Jones, Andrew Lloyd Webber and Pierce Brosnan all have houses nearby.

Graves penned many of his great works here, including *I, Claudius*, and in the 1960s, together with his friend, American painter and archaeologist William Waldren, he set up the **Deià Archaeology Museum and Research Center** (Tue, Thu, Sun 5–7pm; otherwise by appointment tel: 699 957 902).

La Casa de Robert Graves ❹ (Carretera Deià–Sóller s/n; www.lacasade robertgraves.com; Apr–Oct Mon–Fri 10am–5pm, Sat 10am–3pm, Nov–Mar Mon–Fri 9am–4pm, Sat 9am–2pm, Dec–mid Jan Mon–Fri 10.30am–1.30pm) is as it was when he died, and it's worth see-

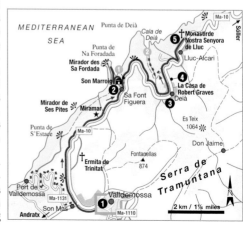

Robert Graves' headstone

Nostra Senyora de Lluc monastery

ing the short film made by the BBC about his life then strolling through the gardens, soaking up the tranquillity and landscape that inspired him.

For something special, it is worth the vertiginous drive down to the Cala Deià to eat at one of the best little fish shacks in Spain, **Ca's Patro March**, see ②.

MONESTIR DE NOSTRA SENYORA DE LLUC

Lluc is the religious centre of Mallorca and home of the island's patron saint. The monastery of **Nostra Senyora de Lluc** (www.lluc.net; daily 10am–5pm, museum Sun–Fri 10am–2pm) is a massive site, and a destination for tens of thousands of pilgrims. But it is of interest to visitors of every creed, for its history, for the architectural interventions of Antoni Gaudí who renovated the basilica, and for its boys' choir – the Escalonia de Lluc. Clad in blue cassocks, they are considered one of the best choirs in Spain and perform renditions of the 'salvo' – a chant intended to protect the island from harm (Mon–Fri 12.30pm, 7.30pm, Sat 11.30am and 7.30pm, Sun 11am, 12.30pm and 5pm in summer, and 7pm in winter).

The monastery was founded in the 13th century when a shepherd found a statue of the black virgin – La Moreneta – in woods nearby. According to lore she had a propensity for disappearing and reappearing again in the same spot she was originally found. After this happened several times she was given a chapel of her own, the Basílica de la Mare de Déu de Lluc.

Ramon Llull's school

Llull believed that the monastery was situated on a sacred site and that the magnetic properties of the earth were particularly strong here, making it an excellent place for study. He dabbled in all sorts of esoteric practices, but believed strongly in education for the masses. The boarding school that was later established on the site is still considered to offer one of the best educations in Spain.

Food and Drink

① SA FORADADA

Crta. Valldemosa Deiá Km 6, Deià; tel: 616 087 499; http://saforadada.com; L and D Apr–Oct only; €€€

Perched precariously on the cliffs, wind-buffeted and wild, this rustic restaurant is an excellent place to drink it all in comfort. The food is simple and cooked over the wood fire; just fine for a quick refuel or a cup of coffee. The paella is especially popular.

② CA'S PATRO MARCH

Cala Deià s/n, Deià; tel: 971 639 137; L; €€€
Cut into the cliffs on a small pebble beach, with driftwood balconies, few places are more romantic. But the attention to spanking fresh seafood is such that Heston Blumenthal declared its Sóller prawns the best he'd ever had. Reservations essential.

The Port de Sóller tram

SÓLLER AND PORT DE SÓLLER

Sóller is one of the nicest towns on Mallorca, yet remains relatively undiscovered as until the road tunnel opened in 1997, it was difficult to reach. It was one of the wealthiest places in Spain in the 19th century thanks to the citrus industry.

DISTANCE: 5km (3 miles)
TIME: A full day
START: Sóller
END: Port de Sóller
POINTS TO NOTE: Sóller is a fantastic alternative to Palma, and this route assumes you will either be staying in the town or the port, or taking the delightful wooden train from Palma. A car is not necessary, as there is a wide range of activities, ranging from soaking up the atmosphere of the Modernista town to hiking in the hills, to spending time on the beach at Port de Sóller. There is a reliable bus service that runs through other villages of the Tramuntana (www.tib. org) daily from 7.30am–8.30pm, which is convenient if you want to hook up with other routes in the area.

In the 19th century Sóller not only produced large quantities of citrus fruits, but shipped them straight from the port to Marseille, generally bypassing Palma altogether – so the wealth generated stayed in this tiny enclave. Fast forward 100 or so years and the imposing Modernista mansions and smart plazas are, if anything, more manicured than ever, while the completion of a multimillion revamp of the Port de Sóller in mid-2011 gave the seafront a much-needed facelift.

Today, both the inland town and the previously rather shabby port attract boutique hoteliers, fine restaurants and smart clubs, where discerning travellers – well-heeled 30-somethings as well as more mature couples – come to get away from it all in style.

If you are driving, leave Palma on highway Ma-11, following signs to Sóller. The journey takes only about 45 minutes, a far cry from the nine-hour trip along the old road, which cut over the **Coll de Sóller**, before the tunnel was built in 1997. Although famed for stunning views back to Palma, the old road was, and still is, vertiginous and slow going, with 28 hairpin bends on the way up and 30 more on the other side.

Sóller

Citrus fruits made the town's fortune

SÓLLER

Even arriving in **Sóller** ❶ has a certain 'wow' factor, since the railway station has its own art gallery showing ceramics by Picasso and a handful of lithographs by Miró. It's not a bad way to start a mini-break in the country. The imposing peaks that surround the little town would give it an almost Alpine air were it not for the huge swathes of orange, almond and olive groves that surround it.

Follow the tram tracks down the hill a short distance to the light-dappled main square, **Plaça Constitució** ❹, dominated by the church of **Sant Bartomeu** ❷ (Mon–Thu 10.30am–1pm, 2.45–5.15pm, Fri–Sat 10.30am–1pm; free), its Modernista facade complemented by the ornate embellishments of the **Banco Santander** ❸ bank on the opposite corner; both were the work of Joan Rubió, who was strongly influenced by Gaudí. The church, in fact, dates from the 13th century, although the main structure is 17th-century Baroque.

Carrer Sa Lluna

Leading off the square is **Carrer Sa Lluna** ❹, a pretty little street of honey-coloured stone with a handful of boutiques and art galleries for browsing. It was so named not because of the face of the moon carved into the side of the house at No. 50, but because of the way the moon comes up over the mountains at one end of it.

Also in Carrer Sa Lluna is another splendid and extremely colourful exam-

> ## The little wooden train
>
> One of the most enjoyable excursions on Mallorca is to take the antique electric train from Palma to Sóller, which departs from the *fin-de-siècle* station in Palma's Plaça de Espanya. It opened in 1912 and has been operating ever since – until the mid-1990s, it was the only comfortable way to get to Sóller. The scenery en route is lovely, especially in February and March when the almond blossom is in full bloom – a trip well worth making. Otherwise you will chug your way serenely through citrus groves and terraced hillsides until the train finally climbs over the mountains via a series of tunnels to descend into the orange-filled Sóller Valley.
>
> Trains leave Palma seven times a day from Mar–Oct (8am, 10.10am, 10.50am, 12.15pm, 1.30pm, 3.10pm and 7.30pm) and five times a day from Nov–Feb (8am, 10.50am, 1.05pm, 3.15pm and 7pm) and take about an hour to reach Sóller; bear in mind that the last train leaves Sóller for Palma at 6.30pm in summer and 6pm in winter. Since 2012, the train makes a stop at the Jardínes de Alfàbia (www.jardinesdealfabia.com; Apr–Oct Mon–Sat 9.30am–6.30pm, Nov, Jan–Mar Mon–Fri until 5.30pm, Sat until 1.30pm) in Bunyola, one of Mallorca's most beautiful gardens, which dates back to Moorish times.

Sant Bartomeu

ple of the Modernista style, **Can Prunera** (www.canprunera.com; Mar–Oct daily 10.30am–6.30pm, Nov–Feb Tue–Sun until 6pm). This grand old townhouse, also the work of Joan Rubió, dates from 1911, and was a family home until 2006. It is a veritable jewel-box, featuring different, brightly patterned tiled floors, stained glass and an ostentatious spiral staircase rising up through the centre of the building. Many of the rooms, such as the dining room and some of the bedrooms, have been left decorated as they would have been during the Belle Epoque, but others have been given over to exhibition space for the work of a wide variety of local and international artists. There is an interesting sculpture garden at the back of the house too, and you could easily spend an hour or two here.

Sóller's other sights

Although Can Prunera is the main sight in town, it is well worth a stroll around to soak up the atmosphere and, if you're lucky, sneak a peek into the walled courtyards and gardens of the splendid old houses. Remember to look up under the eaves – many still exhibit old-fashioned painted roof tiles that depict farm scenes and other aspects

of rural life. Now would also be a good time to stop for a glass of orange juice, for which the town is renowned, for an ice cream at the legendary **Sa Fàbrica de Gelats**, see ❶, or for something more substantial at the flamboyant **La Vila Hotel**, see ❷, another Modernista gem, which serves an excellent lunch.

Museu Balear de Cienciès Naturals

On the western edge of town, the **Museu Balear de Cienciès Naturals** (www.museuciencienaturals.org; Tue–Sat Mar–Oct 10am–6pm, Nov–Feb until 2pm) is a museum dedicated to promoting and preserving the natural assets of the island. The five exhibition rooms include collections of fossils, which are always popular with kids, as well as examples of indigenous flora and fauna.

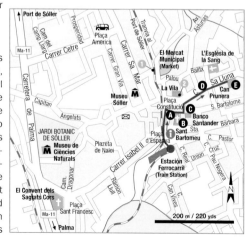

Browse Carrer Sa Lluna

Lunch in Plaça Constitució

Also here is the **Jardí Botànic de Sóller** (www.jardibotanicdesoller.org; Mar–Oct Mon–Sat 10am–6pm, Nov, Jan, Feb Tue–Sat until 2pm), which is strong on Balearic flora with some planting from the Canaries and other Mediterranean islands too. This is a good place to start if you want to know more about what you are seeing when hiking.

A major festival

Sa Fira I Es Firó (www.esfiro.cat) is a lively festival which takes place on the second weekend in May to celebrate Sóller's victory over the Moorish invaders on 11 May 1561. According to local lore, the town was saved by two 'valentes dones' (brave women) who used the same bar they had barricaded their door with to kill their assailants, and successfully

Catch the tram from Sóller to Port de Sóller

sent the corsairs packing. Big and little kids will be enthralled by the exciting battle re-enactments and spectacular evening firework display.

PORT DE SÓLLER

To get to the port, return to the town centre to catch the *tramvia* (tram) to **Port de Sóller ②**. It leaves from the railway sta-

---

Hiking in Sóller

Sóller is probably the best base on the island for walkers, and the ingenious Associació Hotelera de Sóller (www.visit soller.com) is a good way to go about it. With 26 hotels and hostels in their collection, they offer something for everyone and every budget, along with useful facilities ranging from detailed topographical maps to guided hiking trips from Feb–June and Sept–Oct (some of them free). Through the association you can also plan trips if you want to go it alone, or organise a guide to take you through the Tramuntana on a trip lasting several days. There are, however, plenty of easy half-day and day hikes that lead straight out of both the town and the port, which are well signposted and easy to follow. The variety of terrain is spectacular, ranging from ancient cobblestoned trails put in by the Moors to coastal walks where the reward at the end is a jump in the sea, to rolling farmland replete with fruit trees.

tion and the corner of the main square and Carrer Cristobal Colóm every half-hour between 7am and 8.30pm, then at 9.30pm, 10.30pm and 11.30pm, stopping en route where requested; the journey takes about 20 minutes. The old-fashioned open-air wagons run on a line behind some of the village houses, allowing you to get a look at the small gardens, which adjoin virtually every house in Sóller, and you pass through orange and lemon groves and then travel parallel to the main road before entering the little seaside town.

The port has undergone refurbishment, and as of summer 2011 has a wider beach than before, as well as a prettified boardwalk skirting the entire length of the bay. The tram stops every 100m/yds or so along the water's edge, allowing you to get off when you like. The first section – the **Plaça de la Torre** stop – is the best in terms of actual beach, a place to lay your towel and enticing waters in which to bathe. If you keep following the beach around to the left along Passeig de la Platja, you'll eventually arrive at the **lighthouse**, which affords magnificent views over the bay. There is a simple restaurant at the hikers' **Refuge Muleta**, see ❶, or back on the beach at the **Hotel Marina**, which draws diners from near and far for its excellent paella, see ❹, an option for either lunch or dinner.

Santa Caterina

Continuing to the very last tram stop will bring you to the edge of the charming old fishermen's quarter – **Santa Caterina** ❸, always crowded with boats, some of which cruise (in the summer only) to the secluded Tramuntana beaches of Sa Calobra, Na Foradada and the Formentor peninsula. It is also a great place to eat, with several good fish and seafood restaurants.

If you clamber up through these narrow, winding streets you will even-

View over the Port de Sóller

tually get to the **Església de Santa Caterina** and the **Museu de la Mar Sóller** (Oratori de Santa Caterina d'Alexandria; closed for renovation), which provides a fascinating glimpse into the seafaring history of the town. In years gone by it was a magnet for pirates and corsairs, who were lured like moths to a flame to the lucrative little port. Even when the museum is closed, it is worth hiking up here to take a look over the sheer cliffs and inky black water below, imagining what it would have been like for residents of old when ill winds blew and their little town was in danger.

Food and Drink

❶ SA FÀBRICA DE GELATS

Plaça Mercat s/n; tel: 971 631 708, www.gelatsoller.com; L and D; €

No trip to Sóller would be considered complete without stopping at this famous ice-cream-making factory. Although German-owned, this was the first artisan *gelatería* on the island, specialising in orange- and almond-flavoured ice cream made from fruit and nuts grown right here in the Sóller Valley.

❷ LA VILA HOTEL

Plaça Constitució 14; tel: 971 634 641, www.lavilahotel.com; B, L and D; €€

Although there is lots to be said for sitting out on the plaza watching the world go by, the real joy of eating at this chocolate-box hotel is the sheer magnificence of its decor: all floral whimsy and naked nymphs etched into pastel-coloured stained glass. If you prefer to eat alfresco there is also a secret garden at the back when you can dine in the shade of giant palm trees. Either way it's widely considered to serve some of the best modern Mallorcan cooking in town.

❸ REFUGE MULETA

Carretera Es Far de Cap Gros s/n; tel: 971 634 271; L; €

This is a popular stop for hikers coming from Deià along the old GR-221 trail, with stupendous views across the Mediterranean, a picnic area and the kind of hale and hearty fare required after a morning of walking. Think simple, traditional dishes at wallet-friendly prices. Booking ahead is advised, especially at weekends.

❹ HOTEL MARINA

Paseo de la Playa s/n; tel: 971 631 461; www.hotelmarinasoller.com; B, L and D; €€

Probably the most longstanding hotel in the port, the Marina has been run by the same family for four generations. During all this time, one of the highlights of eating here has been the authentic seafood paella that has people returning week after week from as far away as Palma just to get a taste of it. You can't beat eating at a table on the beach-front terrace.

Al fresco dining in Pollença

POLLENÇA AND FORMENTOR

The northernmost corner is a great spot for families. Spend time mooching about the pleasant market town of Pollença and its port, and enjoy the spectacular cliffs and quiet coves of the Formentor peninsula.

DISTANCE: 27km (17 miles)
TIME: A full day
START: Pollença
END: Pollença
POINTS TO NOTE: This route assumes that you will be coming from Palma, although Pollença makes an excellent base for longer stays. The area has plenty of country villas to rent, complete with gardens and swimming pools – many of them more reasonably priced than you might expect – and many of the island's highlights, such as the west coast, Sóller and Palma, are less than an hour away. If you plan to do the route in a day, Sunday sees Pollença at its liveliest, with lots of Spanish families enjoying their traditional lunchtime paella on the seafront in the port.

Getting to Pollença

From Palma, take the Ma-13 motorway to Inca, turning left at the Crestatx junction, which puts you on the Ma-2220 straight to **Pollença ❶**. This is a pretty drive through rolling countryside, but avoids the twists and turns of the more dizzying Tramuntana roads.

The first sight you will see when coming into town is the abandoned hermitage of Nostra Senyora del Puig at 333m (1,090ft). It's worth making a quick detour up here for the view, before heading into the centre of town, clearly signposted 'Centro'. Park where you can and walk along the Via Pollentia to the main square to begin your tour.

POLLENÇA

The central square, **Plaça Major ❹**, is where it all happens, with the tables of numerous bars and cafés spilling into it. It's lively in the evening with lots of people sitting outside to dine alfresco, while the surrounding side streets are good for boutique shopping.

But it is also a town that has several interesting sights. The 14th-century parish church on the square, **La Mare de Déu des Àngels ❺**, was built by the Knights Templar and is one of several religious buildings in the town, including the church of **Nostra Senyora del**

El Calварí steps

The Pont Romà

Roser, as well as the **Sant Domingo** 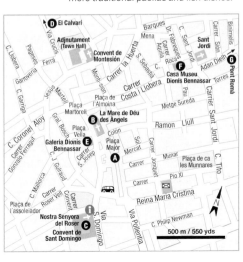 and **Montesión** convents, all built in Baroque style.

El Calварí

None, however, make their presence felt quite like the little chapel of **El Calварí** ⓓ, home to a doll-like figure of Christ that makes an annual outing on Good Friday. The reason for its fame is not so much about Christianity as for the 365 steps that lead up to it, one for every day of the year. Should you be in town at Easter, the *Davallament*, or 'lowering' of Christ from his perch in the chapel of El Calварí to the streets below, is an impressive spectacle and great fun.

Pollença's galleries

The town's laid-back vibe has attracted numerous artists and it now has a handful of decent art galleries, among them the **Galería Dionís Bennàssar** ⓔ (Antoni Maura 11; www.galeriadionis bennasar.com; Mon–Fri 10.30am–3pm, 5–9pm, Sat–Sun 10am–3pm), a nice contrast to the more conservative **Casa Museu Dionís Bennassar** ⓕ (Carrer Roca 14; www.museudionisbenna ssar.com), the home of the celebrated late local painter.

Skirt the town centre by car to Carrer Huerto to pass the **Pont Romà** ⓖ en route to the port. The origins of the bridge are obscure, but it is thought to be part of the canal system built by the Romans in the 2nd century AD.

PORT DE POLLENÇA

The bay of Pollença is shaped like a lobster's claw, with **Port de Pollença** ❷ situated right in the crook. It is lined with restaurants and hotels, many of which have been here since the resort's heyday in the 1950s, and is a good place to break for lunch. Options range from **Stay**, see ❶, one of the finest restaurants in the upmarket marina, to **Bahia**, see ❷, for more traditional paellas and fish dishes.

Idyllic bay on the Formentor peninsula

The resort is bookended by the **Punta de l'Avançada** to the West, which you can get to by walking along the pretty **Paseo d'es Pins** (Promenade of Pines), complete with numerous pocket-sized, sandy beaches and little jetties dotted along it – all ideal for small children.

THE FORMENTOR PENINSULA

The Carretera de Formentor runs parallel to the curve of the waterfront in the direction of the Formentor peninsula. You can join the Ma-2210 from it, and soon afterwards you will find yourself climbing quickly to the **Mirador des Colomer ❸**. The view down to the small island of El Colomer is simply stunning and one of the most photographed on the island.

From here the road dips and ducks through rocky outcrops and pine forest, switching from one side of the peninsula to the other, providing spectacular views of the Bay of Pollença and the Mediterranean. Be warned that it is a bit gnarly, and tough going for anyone who suffers car sickness. It is worth the effort, though, especially if you keep left at the **Formentor Royal Hideaway Hotel ❹**, see ❸, and continue east through the woods towards the **Cap de Formentor ❺**, the northeastern tip of the island.

In the 1950s the Formentor Hotel was the place to see and be seen, and attracted a host of Hollywood A-listers such as Liz Taylor, Audrey Hepburn and Charlie Chaplin, as well as European luminaries like the Duke of Windsor and Grace Kelly, who all

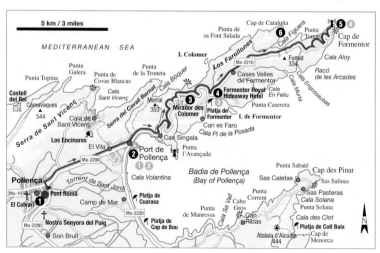

Formentor viewpoint

came to relax here. The beach is wonderful, with fine, powdery sand draped with low-lying palm trees, gentle turquoise waters and fine views across the bay. Although it's unlikely you'll rub shoulders with anyone super-famous these days, it's still a lovely place to kick back in the sun. Get here early for a prime spot on the beach.

Capes and views

On the flat stretch you will pass the crumbling old houses of Cases Velles de Formentor, where one of Pollença's most famous citizens, the poet Costa i Llobera, spent much of his life, and just above **Cala Figuera ❻**, in the distance, a lone pine tree, which inspired one of his most famous poems, *Es Pi de Formentor*.

Continue through the tunnels to the lighthouse. The views out to sea here are tremendous. The first headland visible to the right (southeast) is **Cap des Pinar**, which divides the Badia de Pollença from the Badia d'Alcúdia. Beyond that is the peak of **Cap Ferrutx**, and further towards the horizon is the headland of **Cap des Freu**. This is a great spot for birdwatching in spring and autumn, and on a clear day you can see Menorca, 25 nautical miles east. There is a café at the lighthouse, see ❹, which makes a good place to stop for a drink at the end of a busy day.

Food and Drink

❶ STAY

Carrer Moll Nou s/n, Port de Pollença; tel: 971 864 013; www.stayrestaurant.com; L and D; €€€€

Offering more interesting dishes than many restaurants in the area, Stay is a popular choice for local foodies and visiting yachties. The terrace over the water and its location in the port give it an exclusive, romantic appeal.

❷ RESTAURANTE BAHIA

Paseo Voramar s/n, Port de Pollença; tel: 971 866 562; www.hoposa.es; L and D; €€

With a terrace right on the sand, this is a perfect place for lunch on the beach. Simple grilled fish and rice dishes are the order of the day here, with some token grilled meat options available.

❸ FORMENTOR ROYAL HIDEAWAY HOTEL

Platja de Formentor 3; tel: 971 899 100; www.barcelo.com; B, L and D; €€€

If you are spending the day on the beach, the hotel has a couple of options ranging from more formal restaurant dining to cheaper eats and child-friendly food on the beach. If you don't want to eat then just sip a cocktail while you soak up the sun.

❹ LIGHTHOUSE CAFÉ

Cap de Formentor s/n; tel: 619 748 591; B and L; €

A simple café serving basic snacks such as sandwiches and crisps, soft drinks, beer and coffee, and of course ice cream. It's not the sort of place you make a special trip for, but a fine stop-gap if you just need to refuel.

Alcúdia's 14th-century city walls

BAY OF ALCÚDIA

The Bay of Alcúdia is Mallorca's most popular family resort and gets extremely busy in high season. With lots of water sports, it's great if you're travelling with teenagers and also has child-friendly hotels and restaurants. This route also includes a couple of tips for getting off the beaten path.

DISTANCE: 30km (18 miles)
TIME: A full day
START: Alcúdia
END: Colònia de Sant Pere
POINTS TO NOTE: The beaches here have plenty of family-oriented facilities, ranging from children's play parks to water-sports outlets. The area also has several *ecovias* (bike paths) if you want to go on two wheels.

The great sweep of the Bay of Alcúdia offers everything you could need for a relaxed family holiday, while the ancient walled town of Alcúdia itself and the Parc Natural de S'Albufera both hold plenty of interest when you want to leave the beach behind.

ALCÚDIA

Alcúdia ❶ was originally the Roman town of Pollentia and it later became an important Moorish settlement (Al-Kudia meaning 'town on the hill'). A good chunk of the sturdy walls of the old

medina (town) are still standing, and it is well worth a look around.

The road from Palma brings you along the Avinguda d'Inca; turn right at the roundabout next to the walls (signposted to Port d'Alcúdia), and follow it round to a car park on the left, close to the remains of the Roman city, the **Ciutat Romana de Pollentia**, which was excavated in the 1950s.

You can enter the old city here, straight onto the **Plaça de Jaume Oués Prevere ❹**. The neo-Gothic church of Sant Jaume and a couple of small museums showing Roman and religious artefacts represent the bulk of the sights, but the main square, **Plaça Constitució ❺**, has some lovely Renaissance facades and good restaurants and cafés, and the little town is a pretty place for a stroll, especially if you are there for the Sunday or Tuesday morning markets, when you can shop for picnic food.

The road to Port d'Alcúdia

The road to the port is well signposted from the main town, and on the way there you may like to stop at the **Teatre**

Shopping in Alcúdia

Casa Consistorial

Romà (Roman Theatre). **Port d'Alcúdia** ❷ is not wildly interesting in its own right – and it is very touristy – but it's a good place to have lunch on the beach, such as at **Restaurant Miramar**, see ①, and puts you at the start of the bay proper. It is also the place to get a ferry across to Menorca. From here, follow signs to Can Picafort, which takes you out onto the bay road. You can also walk all the way from the port to Can Picafort on a modern boardwalk.

Platja d'Alcúdia

The Bay of Alcúdia is a 10km (6-mile) stretch of beach sheltered by low dunes. The first section of it, known simply as the **Platja d'Alcúdia** ❸, is perfect for small children, offering abundant amenities, soft, powdery sand and shallow water. Its popularity means there's a good chance that children will find plenty of new friends to play with too.

Parc Natural de S'Albufera

About halfway between the port and Can Picafort you will find the **Parc Natural de S'Albufera** ❹ (www.balearsnatura.com; Apr–Sept daily 9am–6pm, Oct–Mar 9am–5pm; free),

an 800-hectare (2,000-acre) expanse of lagoons and marshes that is one of the best birdwatching sites in the Balearics. It is particularly magical during the spring and autumn migration periods.

Platja de Muro

Sadly, much of the bay is heavily developed, though it is possible to find pockets of loveliness such as the **Platja de Muro** ❺, which is part of the S'Albufera wetlands. It's a bit wilder than

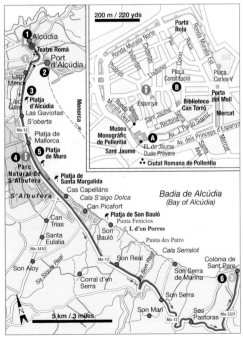

River in the Parc Natural de S'Albufera

the beaches closer to the port and is a great halfway house if you want amenities close by without the crowds. It does have a handful of *chiringuitos* (beach bars, May–Sept only), which cater well for children and make a good lunch stop after a morning on the beach.

COLÒNIA DE SANT PERE

From Can Picafort the Ma-12 swings inwards, cutting out some of the grottier parts of the Bay of Alcúdia. Head back towards the coast just after Ses Pastoras on the Ma-3331, where you will see signs for the increasingly hip little surfer spot of **Colònia de Sant Pere** ❻ on the left. It provides a welcome antidote to the busy resorts, with its low-rise houses clustered around a small fishing port and a pebble beach. Round out a day on the beach with drinks and dinner at **Sa Xarxa**, one of the seaside restaurants here, see ❷.

Water sports

The Bay of Alcúdia is a prime destination for water babies, with activities ranging from sailing and windsurfing to kayaking, water-skiing and scuba-diving. Many places are geared towards students, with courses ranging from a couple of hours up to a week. Most are open April–October.

Funny Beach Alcúdia, located on the beach at Alcudiamar, Ses Fotges and Alcúdia Pins (www.funnybeachalcudia. com) offers giant doughnuts, parasailing and banana flumes. Scuba Mallorca (Carrer d'Elcano 23, Port de Pollença; www.scubamallorca.com) offers PADI courses for children and adults as well as equipment hire and/or dive trips for more experienced divers. Meanwhile, Watersports Mallorca (www.watersports mallorca.com) has its main site on Playa de Muro offering windsurfing, kitesurfing, catamaran sailing and paddle boarding.

Food and Drink

❶ RESTAURANT MIRAMAR

Passeig Marítim 2, Port d'Alcúdia; tel: 971 545 293; www.restaurantmiramar.es; L and D; €€€€

When a place has been around since 1871 you know it is doing something right, and this top-notch seafood restaurant in the otherwise touristy port is a gem. Service is excellent, views are fantastic and the food is always fresh and locally sourced.

❷ SA XARXA

Passeig del Mar s/n, Colònia de Sant Pere; tel: 971 589 251; www.sa-xarxa.es; L and D mid Mar–mid Nov; €€€

A laid-back terrace restaurant with fabulous views across the Bay of Alcúdia. Try homemade tapas including fried baby sardines and baby squid, or sea bass baked in salt with rosemary potatoes.

View over Artà

ARTÀ AND CALA TORTA

Mallorca has a beach for everyone, whether it's a secluded bay, a dune-backed shore or a surfer's hotspot. This itinerary is for serious beach-lovers combining some of the island's secret strands with an up-and-coming country town and lunch at a beach shack serving magnificent seafood.

DISTANCE: 19km (12 miles)
TIME: A full day
START: Artà
END: Artà
POINTS TO NOTE: A rental car is essential; there is no public transport to the remote beaches of the northeast. Try to catch Artà's lively Tuesday morning market and be aware that lunch at the beach hut depends on fair weather (they shut at the first sign of rain and all winter) – get there by 1pm for any hope of a table, as you can't book. It's also a route better suited to early birds than those who like lazy mornings. Both the featured beaches are good for walking (one on sand, the other on cliff paths), so it can be done out of season. There are some memorable places to stay, such as Sa Duaia, Can Simoneta and Cases de Son Barbassa, but early booking is essential.

To get to Artà, take the Ma-15 from Palma to Manacor, and then continue northeast on the same road. It's a straightforward route, clearly signposted all the way, although traffic can get heavy around Manacor, one of the island's main commercial hubs. Once you clear this, the scenery transforms into a series of low, gently undulating hills and lush agricultural land with the sea in the distance. Artà has lots going for it, ranging from stunning architecture to excellent local bistros and good shopping, but it seems it just hasn't been discovered yet by the masses.

ARTÀ

Artà ❶ is hands down one of the loveliest towns on Mallorca, with handsome 19th-century townhouses, boutique shopping and an artsy community all watched over by the **Santuari de Sant Salvador d'Artà ❷** and surrounded by sturdy Moorish walls. It's worth the walk to get a bird's-eye view of the town, before spending a couple of hours exploring the backstreets in search of 'hippie-chic' clothing, designer interiors items and gourmet picnic fare. It's also a great place to eat: try **Café Parisien**,

see ❶. Once they've discovered it people keep coming back, so if you want to stay here, book early.

A wild drive

One of the great joys of this tour is the drive itself, out across the headland that joins Cap de Ferrutx and the Cap des Freu. A more different terrain from that of the Tramuntana is difficult to imagine: wild and barren, windswept and remote.

Drive out of Artà in the direction of Capdepera and follow signs on the left just after the petrol station to Cala Torta. This puts you on the bluff road that rises slowly upwards in a series of knobbly, windswept hills, more Atlantic than Mediterranean, the antithesis of the snug coves of much of the rest of the island, that gives an immense sense of freedom. There's even somewhere to stay – the romantic **Bar Restaurante Sa Duaia** (see page 91) which sits isolated among the hills – and from where there are several wonderful walks across the headland. If you keep going, within 10 minutes of the road starting its descent you come to lovely **Cala Torta** ❸.

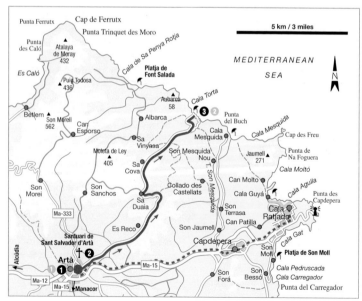

The glorious bay of Cala Torta

CALA TORTA

Popular among the surfing set, naturists and more independent travellers generally, Cala Torta is a scallop-shaped bay with cliff paths connecting it to other, still more secluded beaches. It's got a cool vibe, and the water is beautiful since it gets little by way of passing boats. There is no development whatsoever for miles. To the uninitiated it can seem a little brackish because of the sheer abundance of posidonia, a Mediterranean sea grass, but it's harmless, and indeed desirable since it prevents the beach from eroding. Unfortunately it isn't entirely pleasing to the eye when there's a lot of it washed up on the beach, but you can always find a clear patch for getting in and out of the water, and it tends to remain in the shallows. Seclusion aside, the other reason for visiting Cala Torta is lunch. The eponymous bar, see ②, is nothing more than a wooden shack on stilts, but it serves some of the best grilled fish on the island.

Back to Artà

At the end of the day you have no option but to head back to Artà, but it's the perfect excuse to check out the bars and restaurants, some of which have live music in the evening. Café Parisien and Club Ca'n Moray are both good bets. Or head to Capdepera, which has a surprisingly lively scene for such a small place and some good places to eat. Capdepera's main feature used to be its castle, which affords magnificent views of Menorca over to the east. Today, though, it is known for chic *agroturismos* and hip hotels. Both Capdepera and nearby Cala Ratjada are growing in popularity among more independent travellers. If you want to explore this part of the island both towns are worth considering as off-the-beaten-path bases.

Food and Drink

① CAFÉ PARISIEN

Carrer Ciutat 18, Artà; tel: 971 835 440; B, Br, L and D; €€

Sitting here you could almost be in a bistro in Provence, offering Gallic and Italian-style dishes, jugs of fruity rosé and well-made cocktails. Nostalgic tunes take you back to another era, ranging from Bowie to live jazz bands throughout the summer, and it has a cosy, eclectic vibe that has you feeling like a local in no time.

② BAR CALA TORTA

Platja Cala Torta s/n, Artà; L; €€€

With just four small tables on a tiny wooden deck, and a pint-sized kitchen at the back, this is arguably the smallest restaurant on Mallorca. Yet those in the know travel from far and wide to feast on simply grilled, spanking fresh fish with crisp white wine to wash it down.

Coves d'Artà

CAVES AND GROTTOES OF THE EAST

Mallorca has an extensive network of natural tunnels, caves and grottoes. Carved out by subterranean rivers over millennia, they resemble great man-made cathedrals and castles and are just as jaw-dropping.

DISTANCE: 27km (17 miles)
TIME: A full day
START: Coves d'Artà
END: Coves d'es Hams
POINTS TO NOTE: Although this route doesn't feature any beach time, it links nicely with route 10 (Artà to Cala Torta) and works best if you visit one of the caves in the morning and hit the beach in the afternoon. Note that in high season traffic can be very heavy on the Ma-4023 which links the caves on this route together.

The Jurassic limestone and karst formations that make up considerable chunks of the Balearic Islands are naturally porous. Indeed, neighbouring Menorca is nicknamed 'Swiss Cheese' among scuba-divers for its particularly porous coastal environs. Mallorca's best caves, by contrast, should be explored on foot, and currently there are six networks open to the public. The small but pretty grotto of Gènova, just outside Palma, is handy to have up your sleeve for a rainy day in the city, but to get to the serious stuff you need to head to the east of the island. This route explores the best three examples of nature's architecture.

To get to the Coves d'Artà, drive east from Artà in the direction of Canyamel, bearing left at the Torre de Canyamel. This road leads you straight down to Cap Vermell and the caves.

THE COVES D'ARTÀ

The fact that the **Coves d'Artà** ❶ (Carretera de las Cuevas s/n; www.cuevas dearta.com; daily July–Sept 10am–7pm, Apr–May, June–Oct until 6pm, Nov–Mar until 5pm) are considerably less famous than their counterparts further south is a big part of their appeal: they are much quieter, especially if you time your visit out of season. Yet in some ways they are more spectacular. Less manicured than the prettified caves at Drach, the Coves d'Artà have a grisly history, which still permeates the atmosphere. Some 2,000 Moors hid in the caves after Jaume I's invasion of the island, but his Catalan

troops smoked them out, then slaughtered everyone in one of the bloodiest massacres the island had ever seen. No one came back until the caves were 'rediscovered' in 1876; they are now reputed to have been the inspiration for Jules Verne's *Journey to the Centre of the Earth*.

Visits are conducted in manageable groups, accompanied by rambunctious storytellers who paint a vivid scene. The first thing you'll see on entry is a gigantic stalagmite – 'The Queen of Columns' – rising 22m (72ft) into the air. This is followed by the macabre additions of the 'chamber of hell' and the 'chamber of purgatory'. Things lighten up a bit about halfway past the elephant formations and the 'Diamond Stones', but younger children can find it a bit frightening. Tours last about 40 minutes. There are few facilities here, so pack snacks or head back out of town to the **Porxada de Sa Torre**, see ❶, located in an atmospheric 13th-century tower. Or, if you're looking for luxury, drive into Canyamel, which has the nicest beach in the area, and treat yourself to a lobster lunch at **Cap Vermell Restaurant** see ❷, situated on a jetty positioned over the sea.

PORTO CRISTO

To get to **Porto Cristo** ❷, head back to the Ma-4040 and drive south to Son Severa, where a roundabout exit to the east puts you on the Ma-4023. This takes you straight into the town, the seat of Mallorca's only

action during the Spanish Civil War, when a Republican battleship landed here with a force of 12,000. The troops managed to advance 10km (6 miles) inland, but the Nationalists soon drove them back, and life on the island was once again quiet until the first waves of tourism advanced in the 1960s.

A 1960s holiday resort

In its day, Porto Cristo was a popular holiday resort, although the centre seems a little jaded nowadays. Shops full of tourist tat and cafés selling chips have rather usurped the flavour of the place. However, it is pleasant enough and does retain a certain bucket-and-spade appeal. To get as much joy out of the place as possible, head down to the port on Carrer Burdils, which runs parallel to the beach, down the steps to the fishermen's quay and follow the edge of

Porto Colom

The less well-known little sister of Porto Cristo makes up in charm for what it lacks in size. Centred around two still-working fishing ports, it's a lovely place to have lunch and spend an afternoon strolling along the shore and soaking up the atmosphere. If you can, try to catch it during the Mare de Déu del Carme festival on 16 June, when garlanded fishing boats head out to sea in a floating procession dedicated to their patron saint.

the inlet as it snakes into town. It's not Cala Figuera, but it's a pretty enough place to stretch your legs, and there a couple of interesting architectural features to look at, such as the square at the intersection of Carrer del Mar and Carrer Sant Jordi (a good place to stop for a cup of coffee) and the church of Nostra Senyora del Carme in the square on Carrer Çanglada.

The port is also your best bet for a quick bite, with plenty of places serving simple, family-friendly fare at reasonable prices, see ❶. If you're looking for something special you would be better off going down the coast a bit to Porto Colom or heading for one of the more rural restaurants inland. The area directly south of Porto Cristo boomed in the 1970s and today is almost completely lined with high-rise resorts. It does, however, have one redeeming feature: the Michelin-starred restaurant Bou (see page 102), widely considered to be the best restaurant on the island. For most people, though, the main reason to come to Porto Cristo is to enter the subterranean world of the **Coves del Drach** and the **Coves d'es Hams**.

Coves del Drach

The **Coves del Drach** ❸ (Carretera Cuevas s/n; www.cuevasdeldrach. com; daily Apr–Oct hourly tours 10am–5pm, Nov–Mar tours at 10.45am, noon, 2pm and 3.30pm) to the south of town are Porto Cristo's main attrac-

The quieter Porto Colom

tion, and understandably so. They have been tastefully lit to make the most of the intriguing journey that takes you nearly 2km (1.25 miles) underground, culminating in Europe's largest underground lake, where classical concerts are held and pretty sloops, strung up with twinkling lights, await to ferry you around.

It's all rather romantic in its whimsy, and from the moment you enter there is a certain magic in the air, for these grottoes are straight out of fairy tales, full of mysterious shapes and formations, and weird and wonderful colours. All in all, then, a carefully staged experience, but one that has earned itself the reputation of being Mallorca's top sight. One word of warning: these caves get unbelievably busy and are best visited first thing in the morning or last thing in the afternoon.

Coves d'es Hams

Alternatively you can visit the **Coves d'es Hams** ❹ (www.cuevas-hams. com; daily 10am–4pm, until 7pm in summer), which are about 1km (0.5 mile) north of the town centre. These caves were discovered by speleologist Pere Caldentey in 1905 and feature more of the same, albeit on a smaller scale, complete with a subterranean lake (called the Mar de Venecia) and a floating concert platform, with performances timed to coincide with the tours. If the crowds at Drach are too much, this is a useful second choice.

Food and Drink

❶ PORXADA DE SA TORRE

Carretera Artà–Canyamel Km 5, Capdepera; tel: 971 841 310; L and D; €€€

Decorated with ancient farming implements, this place oozes character from every inch of its historic stone walls. The food is good, too, especially the *lechon* (suckling pig) reared on the restaurant's own farm and slow-cooked over an open fire, and other traditional island dishes.

❷ CAP VERMELL RESTAURANT

Plaça es Pins de Ses Vegues, Canyamel; tel: 971 841 157; www.capvermell beachhotel.com; L, D and drinks; €€€€

Probably the best restaurant on this stretch of coast, it forms part of a smart hotel (see page 92) with a magnificent terrace wedged between the sea and the cliffs. Eat grilled lobster fished from their own tanks, or stop for a glass of champagne.

❸ SA LLONJA

Passeig Moll 1, Porto Cristo; tel: 971 822 859; L and D; €€€

Porto Cristo isn't the best place on earth for food, but this port-side restaurant is a good option. Specialities include fresh fish and seafood as well as paella and other rice dishes. There is a good wine list and the place is child-friendly too.

Gleaming white sands at Es Trenc

ES TRENC AND THE SOUTH

The flat, windswept landscape of the south makes it seem quite wild and isolated. Come here for bracing clifftop walks, to explore rural towns and pretty fishing villages, and to soak up the sun on secluded beaches.

DISTANCE: 29km (18 miles)
TIME: 2 days
START: Sa Ràpita
END: Cala Mondragó
POINTS TO NOTE: This route is spread over two days. If you want to stay longer – and well you might – there's plenty of great-value accommodation, especially around Santanyí, as well as some sweet if basic seaside hotels. If you don't have much time, choose sections of the route such as an afternoon at Es Trenc or a morning at Santanyí market, and make it a day trip from Palma. A car is essential – there is little by way of public transport to these parts – and the route is better suited to couples or young families looking for an alternative side to Mallorca than parents with teenagers looking for entertainment, or anyone wanting to party. It's a good route to take at any time of the year if you're happy to swap sunbathing for rambling.

The quickest way to the south coast from Palma is to take the Ma-19 to Llucmajor, then the Ma-5040 to Campos. The Ma-6030 trunk road heads directly south, and from here the landscape opens out into a series of empty plains dotted with acacia and broom, twisted olive trees and almonds, with huge, piercing blue skies and almost no traffic. No wonder those who have discovered it have kept it to themselves – when you hear talk of 'another' Mallorca, look no further.

SA RÀPITA

This route starts in the dusty backwater town of **Sa Ràpita ❶**, because although Es Trenc is the most famous beach in the Balearic Islands, it is curiously poorly signposted. The easiest option is to go to Sa Ràpita and walk along the beach from there, or to follow signs along a fairly rough A-road to **Ses Covetes ❷**, where there's a large car park, which places you handily about halfway along **Es Trenc ❸** proper. The area is known for its salt production: Flor de Sal d'Es Trenc (www.flordesal destrenc.com) does a range of gour-

met salts including rose, black olive and Mediterranean herb, which are sold in delis and food shops all over the island.

ES TRENC BEACH

If Sa Ràpita is small and sleepy, with little going on beyond the remodelled marina, which does have a handful of good places to eat such as the **Club Nàutic La Ràpita**, see ❶, Es Trenc is a slice of old-fashioned beach paradise. With 3km (2 miles) of pristine white sand backed by low, tousled dunes, you could easily be fooled into thinking you're somewhere in the Hamptons, while the strong breezes that whip up can make it seem more Atlantic than Mediterranean. Rest assured you are

in the right place, as pools of turquoise merging with sapphire-blue waters attest. Eco-activists saved it from development back in the 1970s and ensured that the entire stretch got natural park status while keeping it fairly off-radar from many of the island's visitors.

Much of its appeal is the diversity that comes with the seasons: it is great for refreshing seaside walks if you come out of season, while the central section is beloved in the summer by nudists who seek shelter from the breeze in the dunes. The water is shallow enough for younger children to play safely, while teenagers and grown-ups romp around in the breakers when the wind gets up. You will find a real mix of ages, nationalities, couples and fami-

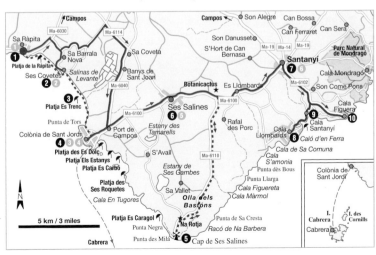

The lighthouse at Cap de Ses Salines

lies here, all with one thing in common: a love of unspoilt beaches.

Happily, then, it is blessedly free of modern beach-going paraphernalia such as jet-skis, banana boats and other aquatic horrors. Facilities amount to a scant handful of *chiringuitos* (beach bars) dotted along its length, some of which rent sun loungers and Balinese-style grass parasols for the day, and serve basic lunches. The best is undoubtedly **Sa Copinya**, see ②, and while you won't find Ibiza-style beach partying, it does have a lazy, laid-back vibe that keeps visitors coming back for more.

COLÒNIA DE SAN JORDI

From Sa Ràpita, drive back inland on the Ma-6030, turn right onto the Ma-6014, and then back down on the Ma-6040 to reach the settlement of **Colònia de Sant Jordi ❹**. Interest is growing in the place, mainly because it is from here that you catch the boat to the island of Cabrera (see page 73), which is often, if somewhat ambitiously, described as the Galápagos of the Mediterranean. The town was established in 1879 as a centre of agriculture and fishing, and it wasn't until the 1950s – as in the rest of the island – that tourists began to arrive. Even then it was a very slow trickle, and although increasing numbers of hotels, bars and restaurants have opened their doors in more recent years, it still has the thrill of a place less travelled.

Although it is no great beauty spot, it has plenty of rugged, seafaring character, and the seafront and port have been spruced up considerably in an attempt to attract the tourist euro. The shallow cliffs that separate the sea from the town make for a pleasant stroll before a lunch stop, maybe at **Port Blau** or **Es Punt**, see ❸ and ❹. If you are around during the first weekend of August, try to catch the annual Colònia de Sant Jordi summer festival, when you will find the streets overflowing with giant paellas, free-flowing beer and cava, and abundant music and dancing.

Secluded beaches

Colònia de Sant Jordi is also the place to head for if you're inclined to seek out the island's more secluded beaches. Heading east away from the town along

Isla de Cabrera

Golden Barrel Cactus at Botanicactus garden, Ses Salines

the sand you will come to several scallop-shaped bays – Es Dolç, Els Estanys, Es Carbó, Ses Roquetes, Es Caragol – each more lovely than the last, and ultimately leading to **Cap de Ses Salines** ❺. It's a full day's walk to get there and back (you can also drive to the lighthouse from Ses Salines), but well worth the effort if you're seeking solitude. Do note, however, that there are no facilities en route.

SANTANYÍ

Heading inland on the Ma-6100 from Colònia, passing through the sweet little town of **Ses Salines** ❻, which is good for a lunch stop at **Cassai**, see ❺, or a visit to **Botanicactus** (www.botanicactus.com; daily summer 9am–7.30pm, winter 10.30am–4.30pm), the largest cactus garden in Europe with more than 1,000 species from all over the world, you reach **Santanyí** ❼, which is the envy of other villages in Mallorca for its looks. The pinkish-hued stone used in the buildings here, besides being the most attractive of all of Mallorca's sandstones, is also the most durable and has been highly coveted at least since the Middle Ages, when it was used in such landmark buildings as Sa Llotja in Palma and the Castellnovo in Naples.

Today Santanyí is the loveliest town in the south, with a groovy, upwardly mobile vibe, thanks to the growing number of artists, writers and affluent second-home owners moving in, looking for a taste of the good life. It's a superb place to shop, with increasing numbers of boutiques selling high-quality goods like linen tablewear and delicate hand-painted ceramics, as well as several good art galleries, and a number of buzzy cafés and restaurants. One of the best is **Anoa Santanyí**, see ❻, praised

Isla de Cabrera

Despite its diminutive size, 'Goat Island', as it is called in English, has a rather dramatic history, starting with the Napoleonic Wars, when it was used as a dumping ground for French prisoners, nearly two-thirds of whom died here. It was also a favoured hideout for the pirates and buccaneers who terrorised the main island. These days it's an altogether more peaceful place. It was declared a national park in 1991, and nature-lovers will get a thrill from the sheer diversity of wildlife: there are seabirds aplenty, a chance of seeing dolphins playing in the surf, and an abundance of the rare Cabrera lizard, now extinct on the mainland. Once on terra firma there is a castle, a museum, a lighthouse and caves to explore, as well as some cute little beaches for swimming and snorkelling (the sea here is teeming with life). There is a small café on the island, but lunch can be provided on board the boat from Colònia de Sant Jordi, or you can take your own picnic. See www.excursions acabrera.es for details.

as much for its friendly ambience as for its lovely food. Saturday is market day and it is well worth visiting specifically for this. Art buffs may want to pay a visit to **Galeria Klee** (Wed and Sat 10am–2pm or by appointment tel: 689 923 290), a contemporary art gallery on Carrer de Palma 28.

Nearby beaches

The nearest beaches are **Cala Llombards** ❽ and Cala Santanyí. The first is a narrow inlet sheltered by tall cliffs and pine trees, with golden sand and a casual, laid-back atmosphere that suits

Santanyí down to the ground. Throughout the summer sardines fresh off the boat are grilled over an open fire at a pop-up beach bar that also serves ice-cold beers to an appreciative crowd who sway to the sounds coming from the bar.

Cala Santanyí ❾ is more crowded because of the long-established Hotel Cala Santanyí (www.hotelcalasantanyi. com), which sits right on the beach. But that means there are better-organised facilities and a generally more family-oriented atmosphere.

CALA FIGUERA

From Santanyí it is a short distance to the picturesque harbour of **Cala Figuera** ❿, which wraps itself around the high, limestone cliffs here. The first recorded data of some kind of settlement here goes right back to 1306, although it didn't develop into a proper fishing village until the 19th century. Park at the top of town and walk down into the harbour, which is one of the unmissable sights on the south coast. Lined by ancient boathouses cut into the cliffs and by pretty, whitewashed fishermen's cottages trimmed with green, it absolutely oozes charm and is a delightful spot for a walk, especially if you arrive as the sun starts to go down, and perhaps before dining alfresco at one of the many restaurant terraces that look over its peaceful waters, such as **Restaurant es Port** (see page 102).

Parc Natural de Mondragó

To the north of Cala Figuera, the wetlands and cliffs of the Parc Natural de Mondragó provide excellent birdwatching opportunities as well as some great walks and postcard-pretty beaches. It can be entered on both the south and north sides, although the south tends to be quieter. It was afforded national park status in 1992 and now comprises rocky, wooded headland with lots of places for jumping into the sea and several picturesque beaches – S'Amarrador, Sa Font de n'Alís (where the information centre is located, and therefore the busiest) and the more secluded Caló des Burgit and Sa Barca Trencada – which all have varying degrees of amenities.

Fishermen's cottages in Cala Figuera

Food and Drink

① CLUB NÀUTIC LA RÀPITA

Explanada del Puerto s/n, Sa Ràpita; tel: 971 640 413; www.restaurantclubnauticsarapita. com; L and D; €€€

This swanky-looking place stands alone at the end of the port, but don't be put off; the prices are more than reasonable and the terrace one of the nicest on this stretch of coast, with excellent sea views. The cooking is likewise superb, offering delicious fresh fish and seafood, perfectly made paellas and service with a big smile.

② SA COPINYA

Platja de Ses Covetes s/n; L; €

Situated midway along Es Trenc (about 20 minutes' walk from Sa Ràpita), a more charming, low-key seaside shack you couldn't hope to find. Excellent fresh grilled sardines and succulent fried calamari served by barefoot waitresses add to the air of bonhomie.

③ PORT BLAU

Carrer Gabriel Roca 67, Còlonia Sant Jordi; tel: 971 656 555; L and D; €€€

This restaurant was opened by the Bauzà family back in 1965, and it continues to be a local favourite today. Buzzing with atmosphere, it's located right between the harbour and the beach and serves mainly Spanish seaside favourites like paella and *fideus*, as well as some child-friendly options.

④ ES PUNT

Avinguda de la Primavera 21, Cólonia de Sant Jordi; tel: 646 752 125 or 681 104 477; www.espunt.net; D and drinks; €€

This friendly local pub with a lively atmosphere is a great place to unwind with a few drinks after a day trip to the Isla Cabrera (they also have rooms if you want to stay the night). Food is basic, but most people come for the music – lots of funk, soul and occasional disco – making it the closest thing the town has to a nightclub.

⑤ CASSAI

Carrer Sitjar 5, Ses Salines; tel: 971 649 721; www.cassai.es; B, Br, L and D; €€

A hip little restaurant with a focus on locally sourced, seasonal ingredients such as grilled cod with aioli, stone-seared duck breast and mountain lamb with herbs. It also does good afternoon teas, handy after brisk walks on the beach out of season.

⑥ ANOA SANTANYÍ

Calle Aljub 32, Santanyí; tel: 971 653 315; www.anoa-santanyi.com; D; €€ – €€€

Within walking distance from Plaza Mayor, this finely decorated restaurant caters mainly for German tourists (even the bill comes in German, not to mention the restaurant's website). A simple menu includes exquisite Mallorcan and international dishes at reasonable prices. Try *sopa de pescado* (fish soup), pasta with prawns or veal steak. Professional and friendly staff.

Statue of St Michael on Felanitx's Sant Miquel church

FELANITX TO PETRA

This route takes you into some of the most obscure parts of Mallorca's hinterland. Travelling the roads that connect the remote sanctuaries and monasteries scattered across the island, you'll cross the market gardens of the plains and ascend onto high plateaux, taking in orchards and olive groves bordered by ancient stone walls.

DISTANCE: 32km (20 miles)
TIME: A full day
START: Felanitx
END: Petra
POINTS TO NOTE: This route can comfortably be done in a day. Should you wish to, however, you can stay overnight in any of these simple monastic cells with nothing but the silence and the stars for company. It's a good Sunday route, with a handful of pleasant hotels along the way if you want to stay longer, notably Sa Plaça Petra Hotel in Petra.

This route will take you through parts of the island that many visitors do not see, where the beauty of the scenery is complemented by the peaceful nature of villages that time seems to have forgotten.

The monasteries themselves are oases of calm, and if you have the time and inclination to stay overnight in one of them, it will be an unforgettable experience.

FELANITX TO SANTUARI DE SANT SALVADOR

Felanitx ❶ is not a wildly interesting town in its own right, although the church of Sant Miquel is impressive and there is a good Sunday market that is particularly strong in terms of local produce. It is also proud to be the birthplace of the artist Miquel Barceló, who had his first exhibition at La Caixa bank here in 1972. His work was immediately coveted and he quickly began to show in other towns across Mallorca and the rest of the world. In 2007 he decorated the chapel of St Peter in Palma's cathedral which portrays, in ceramic clay, the feeding of the 5,000 and the miracle of the loaves and fishes. Fiercely proud of his homeland, in 2013 Barceló did an audio-visual presentation and designed the logo for Mallorca Blackout (www.gobmallorca.com), an environmental campaign to stop over-development on the island.

Traditionally, the town has long been known for its wine and brandy, and it remains largely agricultural today,

Sunday market, Felanitx

Santuari de Sant Salvador

pleasingly devoid of the usual trappings of tourism. If you do stop here, keep an eye out for traditional terracotta water-coolers, which have been made in Felanitx for millennia.

At 516m (1,693ft), the **Santuari de Sant Salvador** ❷ sits at the highest point of the south of the island and straddles two horn-shaped peaks. The lower is occupied by an austere monastery, built in 1348; the higher by a 14th-century fortress, which alas is closed to the public, although part of it has been turned into a charming hotel and restaurant (www.santsalvadorhotel.com). It's a rewarding, if steep walk

(about 3km/2 miles) between the two: a good way to the blow away the cobwebs and a great place for landscape photographers to capture the shimmering early morning light.

Once back in Felanitx, head northwest on the Ma-5100 in the direction of the small town of **Porreres** ❸. Just outside is the tiny **Santuari de Monti-Sion** ❹, worth a stop if you really want to the take the sanctuary theme to extremes – but it's recommended here mainly as a place to stop for lunch. The pedestrianisation of the Avinguda Bisbe Campins sees it heaving with bars and cafés offering light snacks, although it's worth

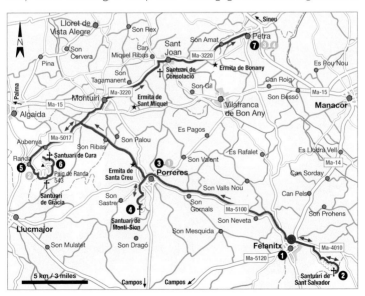

Lunching at the Santuari de Cura

building an appetite for a heartier lunch at the **Restaurant Centro**, see , before continuing on your way.

SANTUARI DE CURA

From Porreres take the Ma-5030 to the Ma-15 motorway, turning left shortly after to join the picturesque Ma-5017 road, following signs for the sleepy, picturesque village of **Randa** ❺, which is said to be the prettiest inland village on the island. The road snakes its way up to the tabletop mountain of **Puig de Randa**, passing stone cottages with pretty, moss-green shutters tumbling over with bright blooms, while tinkling streams go gurgling through. It has an otherworldly ambience, like something from *Lord of the Rings*, not least because the **Santuari de Cura** ❻ – set up by the godfather of Mallorcan literature, Ramon Llull, as a centre for learning in the 13th century – seems like exactly the kind of place a wizard would be proud to inhabit.

Ramon Llull's centre of learning

The sanctuary didn't become a monastery until much later, in the 17th century, and even now it oozes a certain scholastic air. Today it encompasses a small chapel, pretty gardens and a museum dedicated to the life and works of Llull: **Museu del Aula de Gramática Ramón Llull** (daily 10am–1pm, 4–6pm). There is also a café-cum-restaurant. Most visitors just come to admire the views, but you could spend the night (www.santuari decura.com) if you so desired. There are three oratories on the way up the hill, and **Es Recó de Randa** is a good stop for food on the way down, see ❷.

PETRA

Continuing north along the Ma-15, the road sweeps northeast through the pleasing little towns of Montuiri and Sant Joan (just past the Santuari de Consolació) to **Petra** ❼, an unlikely gem in the middle of nowhere. In the last few years Petra has become what you might call a 'boutique' town. Both the church and the museum, the **Casa-Museu Fra Juníper Serra** (www. visitpetramallorca.com/casa-juniper-serra) are worth a look, but mainly to enjoy the pretty garden and as a means of placing the history of Fray Junipero Serra (1713–84) in context.

This Franciscan monk was Mallorca's most famous missionary, and one of the island's best-known sons. The fruits of his labours are particularly prevalent in parts of California, where he founded a number of missions, including the one that is now the city of San Francisco.

Eating in Petra

It is the town itself that is the best place to spend a couple of hours and a great spot for foodies, with several excellent places to eat, as well as its own local winery, the **Bodega Miquel Oli-**

Religious manuscripts in Petra

vera (Carrer Font 26; www.miqueloliver. com; Mon–Fri 10am–6pm, Sat 11am–1.30pm), which has excellent fruity wines made by one of the island's few female wine-makers, Pilar Oliver.

If you are having lunch in Petra, or staying for dinner, **Dolc y Dolc** and **Sa Plaça Petra** are highly recommended, see ❸ and ❹. Petra is one of the top spots on the island for *cuina Mallorquina*, traditional country cooking, particularly at its cool and cavernous *cellers* – old-fashioned bodegas.

Sineu Market

A short detour from Petra along the Ma-3330 takes you to **Sineu**, an agricultural village, which on Wednesdays boasts the oldest market on the island. Dating back to 1306, it is the only one that still deals in livestock and is also a good place to pick up foodie gifts and high-quality crafts. Other than that, the main sight in town is the medieval church, Nostra Senyora dels Àngels. Stop for a coffee in Café Sa Plaça in the main square before heading off.

Food and Drink

❶ RESTAURANT CENTRO

Avinguda Bisbe Campins 13, Porreres; tel: 971 647 547; B, L and D; €€
An atmospheric lunch stop that offers a keenly priced *menú del día* of three courses including a drink, as well as more pricey fish dishes and grills. They also serve pizza and pasta.

❷ ES RECÓ DE RANDA

Carrer Font 21, Randa; tel: 971 660 997; www.esrecoderanda.com; B, L and D; €€
A pretty, 17th-century inn that is especially good on a chilly day in winter, when they light the fire in the dining room. Expect to find hearty country classics such as wood-roasted suckling pig and *arroz brut* (clay-pot rice).

❸ DOLC Y DOLC

Carrer Sol 53, Petra; tel: 971 830 036; L and D; €

Around the corner from Sa Plaça (below), this good pizzeria also does delicious salads, baguettes and desserts – try the blueberry cheesecake. It is super-friendly and serves enormous portions. It's a great place to come after a long day's sightseeing or walking, but be warned that you want to come here really hungry. Excellent value and a nice outdoor terrace.

❹ SA PLAÇA PETRA

Plaça Ramon Llull 4, Petra; tel: 971 561 646; www.petithotelpetra.com; L and D; €€€
This is one of the area's more upmarket restaurants. Sa Plaça has quaint, country-cottage decor and serves staunchly traditional fare. You will be offered dishes such as crayfish and chocolate (try it, it sounds like a strange combination, but is very good) and chicken stuffed with prawns. But do try to save room to savour some of their delectable home-made puddings.

Village of Santa Maria del Camí

WINE COUNTRY

Mallorca is fast making its mark as a serious winemaking region, much of it centred around the rural town of Binissalem, a good base for visiting some of the best and most exciting wineries and getting to grips with the endemic grape varieties while doing some pleasant sipping and swirling.

DISTANCE: 25km (15 miles)

TIME: A full day

START: Santa Maria del Camí

END: Binissalem

POINTS TO NOTE: This route is created for driving, but it could easily be done by bicycle since distances are short and the region is flat. The best time of year to do it is September, when the grape harvest celebrations take place, but if you find yourself here in August, the Bodega Vins Nadal hosts a super jazz festival. With 13 different wineries – details of which can be seen at www.binissalemdo.com – now open to the public, you could easily make the route last a few days or a long weekend. This tour takes in a broad selection to serve as a general introduction to the area.

Wine has been made on Mallorca since Roman times, and the vintages were highly regarded, too, compared by the historian Pliny to the finest wines in Italy. Over time the production of wine spread across the island into the regions of Bunyola, Campos, Felanitx, Manacor, Porreres and Valldemossa, although much of it was wiped out during the phylloxera outbreak in 1899. Up until this point, and unlike the rest of Europe, the island had remained blessedly free of the wine louse, but in the following 100 years production fell from 30,000 hectares (75,000 acres) to a mere 2,000 (5,000). It wasn't until the 1960s that wine production started up in earnest again, and as interest in Spain as a gourmet destination grew in the mid-1990s, so winemakers in Mallorca upped their game. Today they offer some of the most exciting (and expensive) wines in the country, and there is no better place to get acquainted with them. The most important local grape varieties are Manto Negro, Callet and Moll (red) and Premsal Blanco (white). Look out for these on the bottle labels to get a proper taste of Mallorca's distinctive *terroir*.

SANTA MARIA DEL CAMÍ

Away from the coasts, the quiet countryside and ancient towns of the Mallorcan

Bodegas Angel's vineyard

interior have remained largely unaffected by tourism, offering a taste of old-style island life to those who make the effort to go and find it. Take the Ma-13 highway from Palma in the direction of Inca, and within 15 minutes you will see signs to the pretty village of **Santa Maria del Camí ❶** – a good place to fuel up with a strong cup of coffee in the main square before this tour begins.

Macià Batle ❷ (Camí de Coanegra s/n, Santa Maria del Camí; tel: 971 140 014; www.maciabatle.com; guided visits Mon–Sat mid-Mar–Oct 11.30am, 12.30pm, 2pm, 3.30pm and 4.30pm, Nov–mid-Mar at noon, 2.30pm and 4pm) is located just a little way north of the town centre, and

is one of Mallorca's best-known wineries, occupying an impressive position on the plains, with the Tramuntana mountain range rising up behind. The winery is well geared for visits, with a smart tasting room that looks out over the maceration tanks and the vineyards, but the labels themselves are also noteworthy, as each has been designed by a famous artist – both international names and local ones – among them Rebecca Horn, Yannick Vu and Pep Coll. At the other end of the scale, **Celler Sebastià Pastor ❸** (Carrer Paborde Jaume 17, Santa Maria del Camí; tel: 971 620 358; www.sebastiapastor. com; Tue–Fri 8.30am–2pm, 4–8pm, Sat–Mon am only) is a far more modest

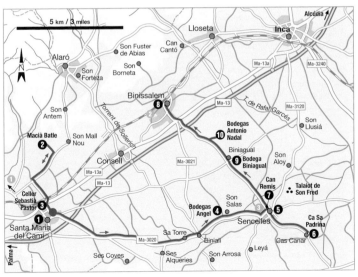

Wine vats

affair, but interesting because here they make wines using only local grape varieties. The wine is simple – table wines rather than great vintages – but an enjoyable variety that is perfect for picnics. If you are in the area at lunchtime, it's worth making a short detour northwest for lunch at the delightful **Moli des Torrent,** see ❶.

SENCELLES

On the road to Sencelles you will pass **Bodegas Angel** ❹ (Carretera Santa Maria–Sencelles Km 4.8; tel: 971 621 638; www.bodegasangel.com; Mon–Fri

10am–5pm), one of the most state-of-the art, modern wineries on the island, which prides itself on excellent new-wave wines, including a stupendous white. For anyone who appreciates small-production boutique wines, this is one not to be missed.

Continue in the direction of the one-horse town of **Sencelles** ❺ and just outside you will find **Ca Sa Padrina** ❻ (Cami dels Horts s/n, Sencelles; tel: 660 211 939 or 646 318 600; http://vinscasa padrina.com; phone in advance to arrange a visit), which is likewise intent on rediscovering traditional winemaking techniques by using only endemic grape varieties and harvesting everything by hand. Again, it's a must for serious wine drinkers.

A traditional winery
Heading directly north out of town, **Can Remis** ❼ (Carrer Sor Francinaina Ana Cirer 14, Sencelles; tel: 971 872 418; Mon–Sat 10am–8pm, Sun until 2pm) is one of the oldest wineries and brandy distillers on the island, dating back to 1870. It makes a striking contrast to the more contemporary facilities you will have visited earlier in the day, and is a good halfway point for breaking for lunch.

BINISSALEM

If you are happy to keep going, continue north to **Binissalem** ❽, which has good eating options and puts you at the heart of wine-growing country. But be sure to save enough energy to stop en route at the **Bodega Biniagual** ❾ (Ap. Correos 5; tel:

Celler restaurants

Most of what you read about Inca is in the context of its leather-working past and its current incarnation as a hub of shoe outlets. The truth is both industries are in decline, and bargains are few and far between. Inca, in fact, is far more interesting as the centre of centuries-old wine *cellers*, which operated much like modern-day wine bars. Most didn't start serving food until the mid-20th century, but once they did, a whole new tradition of *celler* cuisine was born: one that was hale and hearty, featuring local produce in abundance, and restored regional recipes such as roast quail and pork wrapped in cabbage leaves to their place at the top of the island's culinary hierarchy. Come to Inca to eat rather than shop, and you won't leave disappointed.

Entrance to the winery

Chardonnay and Prensal Blanc grapes at Bodegas Angel

678 079 148; www.bodegabiniagual.com; call ahead to arrange a visit), arguably the prettiest winery on the island. The cooperative occupies the whole hamlet of Biniagual and attracts some of Spain's most talented winemakers, so it always makes for interesting drinking. They also produce olive oil.

Just before you reach town, **Bodegas Antonio Nadal** ❿ (Finca Son Roig, Camí de Son Roig, Binissalem; tel: 630 914 511; www.antonionadalros.com; Mon–Fri 9am–1pm, 4–6pm, Sat–Sun by arrangement only) was the first winery on the island to gain D.O. status in 1989. Its wines are still considered to be among the best, and if you treat yourself to a bottle of Magdalena Nadal Estela you will find out why.

And so to Binissalem, the official seat of the D.O. (Denominación de Origen). **Vins Nadal** (Carrer Ramon Llull 2, Binissalem; tel: 971 511 058; www.vinsnadal.com; Mon–Thu 9am–1pm, 3–6pm, Fri am only, call ahead) offers superb wines at reasonable prices. They also stage jazz concerts in the cellars in the summer, with great food and wine. But no visit is complete without a stop at **José Luis Ferrer** (Carrer Conquistador 103; tel: 971 511 050; www.vinosferrer.com), probably the island's most famous winery. The distinctive orange label of their crianza is the house wine of choice for restaurants all over Mallorca.

Thus lubricated, you will be glad to know there are several good places to eat in Binissalem, and it's a great place to round off the day either with a full dinner or with drinks on the square: try **Café Singló** or **Sa Cuina de N'aina**, see ② and ③.

Food and Drink

① MOLI DES TORRENT

Carreterade Bunyola (Ma-2020), Santa Maria del Camí; tel: 971 140 503; www.molides torrent.de; L and D, closed Wed–Thu; €€€

On the western outskirts of town, this beautiful restored windmill is a lovely place to dine alfresco in the summer and well worth the detour. The German-run restaurant focuses on seasonal regional cuisine and features the likes of prawns with potato salad followed by apple strudel. There is a good selection of Mallorcan wines and also German beers.

② CAFÉ SINGLÓ

Plaça Església 5, Binissalem; tel: 971 870 599; http://singlo.restaurantesok.com; B, L and D; €€

This upmarket café-restaurant with a pleasant terrace on the main square is very much a local meeting point, whether it's for coffee first thing in the morning, a top-flight three-course *menú* for lunch, or drinks in the evening.

③ SA CUINA DE N'AINA

Carrer Rafal 31, Sencelles; tel: 971 612 178; www.sacuinadenaina.com; L, D, closed Mon D and Tue; €€

Family-run small restaurant set around an attractive interior courtyard. The food, like the surroundings, is traditional: roast suckling pig and lamb are the house specialities. Homemade fig ice cream is a winner for dessert.

DIRECTORY

Hand-picked hotels and restaurants to suit all budgets and tastes, organised by area, plus select nightlife listings, an alphabetical listing of practical information, a language guide and an overview of the best books and films to give you a flavour of the city.

ACCOMMODATION

Mallorca has a wide range of accommodation, ranging from trendy boutiques in Palma to chic farmhouse accommodation inland. Hotels are rated from one to five stars but bear in mind that the rating is related to the facilities offered and not the quality of service.

Small family-run establishments in the lower categories can be more comfortable than large resort hotels: try **Little Hotels** (tel: 0117 230 3500 (UK); www.littlehotels.co.uk) and **Secret Places** (tel: 214 647 430; www.secret places.com). For rural hotels, villas and apartments see **Rural Hotels Mallorca** (tel: 0203 239 4983 (UK); www. ruralhotelsmallorca.com). Most deluxe accommodation is clustered around the west coast, while you can get great package deals if you head east. Some hotels close for a few months off season, but those that remain open tend to have good offers. This list only covers areas included in the routes, and some areas are stronger than others in terms of places to stay. The Bay of Alcúdia, for example, caters mainly for package tourists, so we recommend staying in nearby Pollença if you want a different experience.

The following guide indicates prices for a standard double room in high season, but should be used as an approximate guide only. VAT (IVA) at 10 percent and breakfast are sometimes included in a quoted rate, but it is wise to check. Prices do not include the new eco-tax introduced in 2016, applying to visitors and residents over 16 (costing up to €1 a night in low season and €2 in high).

If you are planning on staying more than a few days it might be worth renting an apartment: try www.airbnb.com, www.apartments-spain.com, www.house trip.com, www.ownersdirect.co.uk and www.holidaylettings.co.uk. Walkers will find plenty of basic refuges and hostels but campsites are few and far between. Those seeking peace and quiet should consider staying in a monastery. Tourist offices will have details of all kinds of accommodation.

Price for a double room for one night in high season:

€€€€ = above 250 euros
€€€ = 125–250 euros
€€ = 75–125 euros
€ = below 75 euros

Palma

Hotel Almudaina
Avinguda Jaume III 9; tel: 971 727 340; www.hotelalmudaina.com; €€€
Comfortable and moderately priced with obliging staff, the Almudaina is on Palma's foremost shopping street. Established in 1972, it was completely

Hotel Bon Sol's opulent lobby

renovated 20 years later. There are magnificent views across the city and bay from the terrace, bar and upper-floor rooms.

Hotel Bon Sol
Passeig de Illetes 30; tel: 971 402 111; www.hotelbonsol.es; €€€

This quirky family-run hotel is a delight, about a 20-minute taxi ride from the centre. Heavy Spanish furnishings in the lobby are complemented by light, airy bedrooms; gardens and terraces cascade down to the sea; and there's a private beach. Yoga classes and spa facilities are included in the price.

Hotel Born
Carrer Sant Jaume 3; tel: 971 712 942; www.hotelborn.com; €€€

A taste of the Palma that was, this lovingly renovated palace is right in the heart of the city and oozes atmosphere, though some rooms are showing their age. Regardless, it's spotlessly clean and the open-air courtyard where breakfast is served is hard to beat.

Hotel Convent de la Missió
Carrer de la Missió 7; tel: 971 227 347; www.conventdelamissio.com; €€€

This stylish hotel, set in a converted 17th-century convent in the old quarter, has minimalist all-white rooms, a roof terrace, solarium and steam rooms, and an excellent restaurant, Marc Fosh. The art gallery, housed in the old refectory, hosts temporary exhibitions

Hotel Feliz
Avinguda de Joan Miró 74; tel: 971 288 847; www.hotelfeliz.com; €€€

One of the grooviest newcomers to arrive on the scene for a while, Feliz has a Scandinavian aesthetic boosted by lots of bright colour woven into an old 1960s apartment block. The 'fish tank' swimming pool on the terrace is fun, while the ample lounge stuffed with squishy sofas is a great place to chill out at night.

Hotel Portixol
Carrer Sirena 27, Portixol; tel: 971 271 800; www.portixol.com; €€€€

The hotel of choice for hip young things wanting to hang out on the beach, Portixol ticks a lot of boxes: sexy lounge and cocktail bar, great food, a pool to be seen in, plentiful pampering treatments. The seafaring theme in the bedrooms extends to binoculars for watching the wildlife.

Palacio Ca Sa Galesa
Carrer Miramar 8; tel: 971 715 400; www.palaciocasagalesa.com; €€€€

Housed in a grand, meticulously restored 17th-century palace, this tiny hotel (only 12 rooms) is furnished with antiques, has a courtyard with fountain, and an indoor pool.

Palau Sa Font
Carrer Apuntadors 38; tel: 971 712 277; www.palausafont.com; €€€

A delightful hotel in a 16th-century episcopal palace, with 19 individually decorated rooms – those at the back are quieter, but this is the quiet end of the busy street. Buffet breakfast included.

Puro Hotel

Carrer Montenegro 12; tel: 971 425 450; www.purohotel.com; €€€€

Arguably the city's trendiest hotel, Puro has designer chic emanating from every faux animal skin-covered pouf or sleek leather armchair. It pays to be a creature of the night when staying here – it's somewhere to party rather than chill out. The hotel also has a tasteful beach club just beyond Ciutat Jardi.

Hostal Ritzi

Carrer Apuntadors 6; tel: 971 714 610; www.hostalritzi.com; €

One of Palma's few budget options, the Ritzi occupies an attractive old townhouse just off the lively Passeig de Born. It has 17 rooms, ranging from en suite doubles to bunk-bed dorms for friends sharing.

Hotel San Lorenzo

Carrer San Lorenzo 14; tel: 971 728 200; www.hotelsanlorenzo.com; €€€

This enchanting little hotel (only nine rooms) is always booked well in advance. The bright rooms are individually decorated in traditional Mallorcan style; all have balconies and some have garden access. If you don't

fancy heading to the beach there is a small pool.

Hotel Tres

Carrer Apuntadors 3; tel: 971 717 333; www.hoteltres.com; €€€€

A sleek, contemporary renovation of an aristocratic townhouse, Tres attracts a more grown-up crowd than Puro, without being stuffy. Rooms are stylish and spacious, the central courtyard and lounge are both great places for breakfast and hanging out, and two roof terraces give splendid city views.

Andratx to Banyalbufar

Hotel Brismar

Almirante Riera Alemany 6, Port d'Andratx; tel: 971 671 600; www.hotelbrismar.com; €€

This comfortable and simple seafront hotel is a bargain given the coveted location. Ask for a room with a view of the harbour, although these are the noisiest. The restaurant serves traditional Mallorcan food and has lovely views across the port.

L'Escaleta

Carrer del Porvenir 10, S'Arracó; tel: 971 671 011; www.hotelescaleta.com; €€

Beautifully converted old schoolhouse located a short distance inland from Sant Elm. Rooms are individually furnished in traditional style, plus there is a pool and a lovely garden where dinner is served on some evenings. Ideal for hikers and cyclists. Breakfast included.

Finca S'Olivar

Carretera Ma-10 Km 93.5, Estellencs; tel:
971 618 593/629 266 035; www.fincaolivar.
org; €€

Gorgeous *agroturisme* set in a 15-acre
private valley with wonderful views over
the coast. The self-catering accommodation (breakfast available) is in two
traditional stone houses and two cottages. There is an idyllic infinity pool
with a terrace.

Hotel Mar-i-Vent

Carrer Major 49, Banyalbufar; tel: 971 618
000; www.hotelmarivent.com; €€€

This family-run hotel was one of the
original hotels to spring up on the west
coast. The bedrooms are light and airy if
fairly basic, but the main reason to stay
here is to take advantage of its extraordinary clifftop pool and dazzling sea
views. Closed Dec–Jan.

Hotel Rural Nord

Plaça d'es Triquet 4, Estellencs; tel: 971
149 006; www.hotelruralnord.com; €€

This traditional stone village house is
built around a courtyard that has been
revamped with a designer's touch.
Sunny bedrooms, local produce and a
restored olive mill for drinks at the end
of the day deliver far more than you
would expect from the price tag. A real
bargain. Closed Nov–Jan.

Villages of the Tramuntana

Hotel Son Palou

Plaça de la Església s/n, Orient; tel: 971 148
282; www.sonpalou.com; €€€

Tranquil, beautiful and stylish, Son
Palou is regularly voted best base on
the island by hikers, so book well in
advance if you want to stay here. It has
cosy lounges (complete with crackling
fires in winter), romantic bedrooms,
rambling gardens, a huge pool and a
superb restaurant specialising in traditional country cooking.

Valldemossa to Lluc

Hotel Miramar

Carrer Ca'n Oliver s/n, Deià; tel: 971 639
084; http://pensionmiramardeia.com; €€

Set above the main road up a narrow
track, this pleasant little *hostal* has
a cavernous entrance hall and nine
rooms (not all have bathrooms). Breakfast, which is included in the price, is
served on the terrace. The walls are
adorned with works by artists who have
stayed there over the years.

Es Molí

Carretera Valldemossa–Deià s/n; tel: 971
639 000; www.esmoli.com; €€€€

Es Molí is a magical place occupying
several acres of lush gardens at the
foot of Es Teix mountain, overlooking
the sea. It has a contemporary feel,
personal service and romantic ambience. Access to a private beach – Sa
Muleta – is an added bonus. Closed
Nov–mid-Apr.

Belmond La Residencia

Son Moragues, Deià; tel: 971 639 011;

www.belmond.com/la-residencia-mallorca/; €€€€

Probably Mallorca's most famous hotel, La Residencia is loved by visiting celebrities and European glitterati. Set in two chic and elegant 16th-century manor houses, this is the place to be if you value privacy and a hotel capable of satisfying your every whim. The modern Mallorcan restaurant El Olivo is one of the best in Spain.

S'Hotel d'es Puig

Es Puig 4, Deià; tel: 971 639 409; www.hoteldespuig.com; €€€

A fantastic option of the chic and cheap variety, this small village hotel has sleek, contemporary rooms, a pool and flagstone terrace, fabulous views and friendly, family service. It has also had a host of illustrious guests over the years (Robert Graves used to put his pals here) and retains a bohemian atmosphere. Closed mid-Nov–Feb. Breakfast included.

Sóller and Port de Sóller

L'Avenida

Gran Via 9, Sóller; tel: 971 634 075; www.avenida-hotel.com; €€€€

One of the hippest boutiques on the island, L'Avenida has just 12 luxury suites, each more glamorous than the last. Elsewhere, communal areas are dripping in luxury, while the arcaded terraces around the pool are the height of sophisticated elegance. This place offers a real treat and is a fan-

tastic choice for romantic weekend getaways.

Hotel Esplendido

Es Traves s/n, Port de Sóller; tel: 971 631 850; www.esplendidohotel.com; €€€€

The grooviest hotel on the seafront, Esplendido is owned by the same people as the Portixol in Palma and despite its size, it has a boutique appeal. It reopened in the spring of 2011 after a major revamp with the addition of a spa, firmly establishing itself as the place *du jour* among style-savvy travellers.

Jumeirah Port Sóller Hotel & Spa

Carrer Belgica s/n; tel: 971 637 888; www.jumeirah.com; €€€€

This dazzling five-star hotel has been described as one of the finest in the Mediterranean. With stunning cliff-top views, two gourmet restaurants, four bars, two swimming pools and a spa, who are we to argue? The Lighthouse Suite has its own spacious terrace complete with jacuzzi.

Es Port

Carrer Antonio Montis s/n, Port de Sóller; tel: 971 631 650; www.hotelesport.com; €€€

This meticulously restored 17th-century stone farmhouse is hugely popular with hikers. With several living rooms built around an ancient olive press, rambling gardens, two huge pools (outdoor and in) and crackling fires in the winter, you

The luxurious Belmond La Residencia has a wonderful setting in Deià

can see why so many people keep coming back for more.

Pollença and Fortmentor

Hostal Bahia

Paseo Voramar s/n, Port de Pollença; tel: 971 866 562; www.hoposa.es; €€€

An attractive and friendly establishment in a 19th-century summer home, with an inviting terrace, right by the sea. Closed Nov–Feb.

Formentor Royal Hideaway Hotel

Platja de Formentor s/n, Formentor; tel: 971 899 100; www.hotelformentor.net; €€€€

Overlooking the beach, this classic hotel has been around since the 1950s, when it was something of a haven for travelling stars; Ava Gardener and Liz Taylor have both stayed here. These days it attracts business and leisure travellers for its spot on one of the most beautiful beaches on the island.

L'Hostal Pollença

Carrer Mercat 18, Pollença; tel: 971 535 282; www.pollensahotels.com; €€

This place is excellent value for money: it's really a B&B that's gone upmarket, with a lively ambience, colourful rooms all with en suite bathrooms, and a groovy retro public room for trading books and gossiping. Breakfast is served at the sister-hotel around the corner, the Hotel Juma on the main square.

Son Brull

Carretera Palma–Pollenfa Km 49.8, Pollença; tel: 971 535 353; www.sonbrull.com; €€€€

One of the most stylish boutiques on the island, Son Brull is a monastery that has been converted into a shrine to contemporary minimalism. Perfect for design aficionados, yet unexpectedly welcoming to children; expect lots of clean lines, futuristic food and impeccable service.

Artà and Cala Torta

Bar Restaurante Sa Duaía

Carretera Artà–Cala Torta Km 8; tel: 658 958 890; www.saduaia.com; €€

A secret hideaway on the bluff above Artà, this place attracts an alternative crowd who enjoy a bit of splendid isolation. Apartments are rustic but comfortable, it has a great pool, and though the food is fairly ordinary, the wildness of the terrace makes it one of the best on the island.

Hotel Casal d'Artà

Carrer Rafael Blanes 19, Artà; tel: 971 829 163; www.casaldarta.de; €€

A good budget option, this friendly townhouse at the top of town is a delight. Typical island decor goes well with a laid-back vibe, while a sunny dining room and terrace make breakfast a time to linger. The roof is a wonderful place to end the day with a glass of wine. Breakfast is included.

Cases de Son Barbassa

Carretera Cala Mesquida s/n, Capdepera;
tel: 971 565 776; www.sonbarbassa.com;
€€€

This chic rural retreat is like the new-wave *agroturismos* of Ibiza: a collection of spacious suites built of stone and wood spread across several olive groves, a pool area surrounded by draped day beds, fantastic food and the sensation that you're miles from anywhere. Breakfast is included.

Hoposa Niu

Carrer Cala Barques s/n, Cala San Vicenç; tel: 971 530 512; www.hoposa.es; €€€

This pleasant, owner-managed hotel overlooking the lovely cove of Cala Sant Vicenç was upgraded in 2015. Facilities include terraces, bar and an excellent restaurant specialising in fish and lobster. Reserve well in advance. Closed Nov–Mar.

Caves and Grottoes of the East

Can Simoneta

Carretera Artà–Canyamel Km 8, Capdepera;
tel: 971 816 110; www.cansimoneta.com;
€€€€

A spectacularly located boutique hotel occupying several acres of cliff-top above the sea. Inside, think cool minimalism, outside manicured lawns, hammocks and a staircase to a private beach. With just eight rooms, service is highly personalised – perfect for a romantic getaway or honeymoon. Breakfast included.

Hostal Porto Colom

Carrer Cristófol Colom 5, Porto Colom;
tel: 971 825 323; www.hostalportocolom.com; €€€

Situated right by the port, this pleasant hotel in an ochre-coloured building offers comfortable accommodation with bright contemporary furnishings. The Mediterranean restaurant has a lovely terrace and the first-floor cocktail bar has live music on Thursdays and Sundays.

Cap Vermell

Plaça es Pins de Ses Vegues 1, Canyamel, Capdepera; tel: 971 841 157; www.capvermellbeachhotel.com; €€

This 1970s-style block on the edge of the sea has a certain Americana retro appeal, with acres of glass and a bleached-wood dining and lounge area. Rooms are more basic, but the terrace is fantastic (as is the food), and it's not a bad little beach spot for the price.

Es Trenc and the South

Hostal Colonial

Ingeniero Gabriel Roca 9, Colònia de Sant Jordi; tel: 971 655 278; www.hostal-colonial.com; €

A basic but pleasing little place in a quiet fishing village, this *hostal* is big on family seaside appeal, with its own ice-cream parlour and a huge range

Looking out over Artà

of hot chocolate. It's also one of the cheapest places to stay on the island. Breakfast included.

S'Hotelet de Santanyí

Plaça Major 23, Santanyí; tel: 971 653 583; www.hoteletsantanyi.com; €€€€

This smartly renovated townhouse is a welcome addition to Santanyí's hip village scene. Crisp white linen against honey-coloured stone make for soothing weekends away, while the lively central plaza location gives a sense of being at the heart of things.

Felanitx to Petra

Sa Bassa Rotja

Finca Son Orell, Camino Sa Pedrera s/n, Porreres; tel: 971 168 225; www.sabassarotja.com; €€€

A 13th-century country mansion set in large grounds, with sports facilities, a spa and a restaurant using locally produced ingredients, plus live music on Saturday nights and a barbecue on Sundays. Rooms are furnished in contemporary Mallorcan style. It's ideal for a relaxing or active short break.

Son Bernadinet

Carretera Campos–Porreres Km 5.9; tel: 971 650 694; www.son-bernadinet.com; €€€

A lovely manor house with minimalist decor, surrounded by almond orchards, with its own vegetable gardens, and a log fire to warm you in winter. It feels miles from anywhere, but it's only 15 minutes' drive to the nearest beach.

León de Sineu

Carrer dels Bous 129, Sineu; tel: 971 520 211; http://leondesineu.com; €€

An elegant, antique-furnished hotel with large airy rooms, close to the central square in this attractive old town. There's a welcoming atmosphere and a good restaurant, Sa Boveda, which serves Mallorcan cuisine and has a wide selection of wines. The pool is in a shady garden.

Es Reco de Randa

Carrer Font 21, Randa; tel: 971 660 997; www.esrecoderanda.com; €€

This is a sweet country hotel with old-fashioned rooms and plenty of soul. It's a pleasant base if you want to get off the beaten path a little, and features some nice extras like live music and paella nights through the summer. Breakfast included.

Wine Country

Casa del Virrey

Carretera Inca-Sencelles Km 2.4, Apto Correos 490; tel: 971 881 018; www.casadelvirrey.net; €€€

This old privateer's mansion has been turned into a comfortable country-house hotel where mod cons meet traditional furnishings. There is a restaurant, serving Mallorcan cuisine, and a pool.

RESTAURANTS

When it comes to eating out in Mallorca there's plenty of diversity, though certain areas are much stronger than others. As in most cities, Palma has something to suit a range of tastes and budgets, but once you get outside urban areas it helps to know what you are doing. The restaurants selected follow, roughly, the routes outlined in the walks and tours, but in some cases it's worth travelling a bit further to eat well. You eat much better on the southeast coast than the northeast, and it is worth making the detour if food is the main purpose of your trip.

Opening hours, especially in rural areas and depending on the season, can be a bit erratic. If you want to be sure, it pays to call in advance.

Eating out is no longer particularly cheap, though there are some bargains to be had, and these have been highlighted as much as possible.

Palma

13%
Carrer Sant Feliu 13a; tel: 971 425 187;

> Price for a two-course meal for one with a glass of house wine:
> €€€€ = above €40
> €€€ = €25–€40
> €€ = €15–€25
> € = below €15

www.13porciento.com; L and D; €–€€
Just off Passeig des Born, this attractive wine bar serves excellent salads and plates of ham and cheese as well as fish and meat courses and an excellent variety of wine by the glass or bottle. Good-priced tapas menu for two (or more). Closed Sun lunch.

Basmati
Carrer Caro 7; tel: 971 710 387;
www.restaurantebasmati.com; L and D,
closed Sun; €€
If you fancy a change from Mallorcan food, head to this family-run Indian restaurant in the Los Geranios shopping centre. The menu changes daily and there are plenty of options for vegetarians. The Peshawar naan bread made with dried fruits, honey, coconut and almonds is delicious.

Bon Lloc
Carrer Sant Feliu 7; tel: 971 718 617;
www.bonllocrestaurant.com; Mon–Sat L,
Tue–Sat D; €
This vegetarian restaurant has been around since the 1970s, and continues to draw a crowd for its set-price lunch menu. The food is inventive and healthy, ranging from wholemeal bread with home-made soups to more substantial pasta and bean dishes. The atmosphere is convivial thanks to lots of longstanding regulars.

Marc Fosh is one of Mallorca's best restaurants

El Bungalow

Carrer Esculls 2, Ciutat Jardí; tel: 971 262
738; www.rtebungalow.com; Tue–Sat L and
D, Sun L only; €€€

Ask any chef in Mallorca their favourite fish restaurant and at least half of
them will come back with this place.
Little more than a stone shack on the
beach, it serves fish just the way it
should be: fresh and simply grilled –
and it's just 15 minutes from central
Palma.

La Bóveda

Carrer Botería 3; tel: 971 714 863;
www.restaurantelaboveda.com; Mon–Sat
L and D; €

This iconic Palma tapas bar is the place
to go to rub shoulders with local people and tuck into plates of maple-sweet
jamón Ibérico, slabs of Manchego
cheese, *pimientos de padrón* (sweet,
and occasionally spicy fried green peppers) and heaps of local seafood. Sit at
the bar or on the terrace and enjoy with
an ice-cold *caña* (small draught beer) or
a glass of the local wine.

Caballito del Mar

Passeig de Sagrera 5; tel: 971 721 074;
http://caballitodemar.info; L and D; €€

The place to go for fish and shellfish cooked to suit your requirements.
There's an outside terrace just around
the corner from lively Plaça Sa Llotja but
it's separated from the waterfront by the
busy main road. The paellas and *frituras*
are always popular.

Celler Sa Premsa

Plaça Bisbe Berenguer de Palou 8; tel: 971
723 529; www.cellersapremsa.com; Mon–
Sat L and D; €€

This is a real institution, which has
been operating for 60 years. Great
ambience and good, filling, everyday
Mallorcan classics. Closed Sat and
Sun in July and Aug.

Japonice

Carrer Unió 2; tel: 971 404 060;
www.japonice.com; L and D; €€

This sushi restaurant has plenty to offer
carnivores too. For example, there is
bull steak wrapped in rice and topped
with a slice of chicken liver or cheese
tempura and vegetarian *maki* for non-
meat eaters. The desserts are quite
something – choose from cheese cake
with red fruits or a chocolate brownie.

Safrà 21

Carrer Illa de Corfú 21, Ciudad Jardin; tel:
971 263 670; www.safra21.com; Mon–Sat
L, Thu–Sat D; €€

At lunchtime this restaurant specialises in serving traditional rice dishes; in
the evening it becomes Mallorca's first
'Bistronomic' restaurant, focusing on
top-quality cuisine at reasonable prices.
Closed Sun.

Marc Fosh Restaurant

Carrer Missió 7a; tel: 971 720 114; http://
marcfosh.com; L and D, closed Sun; €€€€

Marc Fosh is one of Mallorca's most brilliant chefs. A staunch proponent of local

produce, his fresh take on traditional recipes – like rice with *sobrasada* (the local pork sausage generously laced with paprika) – ensures intensely satisfying eating, and his flagship restaurant is just the place to try it. For a taste of Fosh on a budget go for the bargain three-course lunch (€27.50), or check out one of his other two branches: Fosh Lab (Carrer d'En Morei 5; tel: 971 595 301), and Fosh Kitchen (Carrer d'Orfila 4; tel: 971 721 354).

Tast Avenidas

Avinguda Comte de Sallent, 13; tel: 971-101 540; www.tast.com; L, D, closed Sun; €€

Award-winning creative tapas in contemporary surroundings. Try the veal with Roquefort or stone-cooked steak.

Andratx to Banyalbufar

Alfresco

Asociación Cultural Sa Taronja, Carrer Andalucía 23, Andratx; tel: 622 616 109; www.limonychelo.com; Fri–Sat D; €€

Something of a well-kept secret, this place works for all seasons. Lushly planted gardens are magical in the summer, while the cosy, fire-lit dining room is a boon in winter months. Live music is staged throughout the year, along with wine-tastings and other cultural events, and the food is superb, much of it home-grown and organic.

Son Tomás

Carrer Baronia, 17, Banyalbufar; tel: 971 618 149; L and D, closed Tue; €€€

This region isn't particularly strong when it comes to dining, but Son Tomás has enjoyed a sterling reputation since the mid-1980s for its sturdy Mediterranean cooking. It buzzes with atmosphere, and the fish soup, paellas and *fideus* are all firm favourites. Harder-to-please customers insist that the views are better than the food.

Villages of the Tramuntana

Ca Na Toneta

Carrer Horitzó 21, Caimari; tel: 971 515 226; www.canatoneta.com; L and D; €€€

Like a little dolls' house, Ca Na Toneta and its creators, Maria and Teresa Solivellas, ooze charm. The delightful dining room makes a fitting backdrop for dishes made from organic products that they grow themselves. They serve only a six-course tasting menu, which changes weekly to reflect the nuances of the seasons. It's one worth travelling for. See website for opening days and times.

Dalt Muntanya

Carretera Bunyola–Orient Km 10; tel: 971 615 373; www.hoteldaltmuntanya.com; L and D; €€€

Part of a hotel of the same name, this restaurant has a fabulous terrace from which to take in the scenery over a hale and hearty menu of hikers' favourites. Plenty of vegetable-rich starters, but the stars are slowly roasted leg of lamb or suckling pig: both superb.

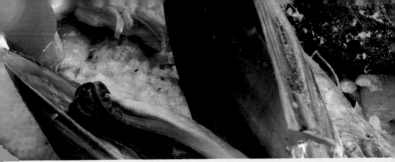

The traditional rice dish paella

Mandala
Carrer Nueva 1, Orient; tel: 971 615 285; L and D, closed Mon and Sun evening; €€€

This romantic, cottage-style spot combines the best Mallorcan ingredients with flavours from Asia to great effect, and is an unusual find here in the mountains. Popular in the cooler months when people are spending several days exploring local trails, dishes range from duck breast with plums to fish curries and spicy puddings.

Traffic at Can Xim
Plaça de la Vila 8, Alaró; tel: 971 879 117; www.canxim.com; L and D; €€€

Despite the unlikely-sounding name, this is a charmer, with its ancient wood beams and rustic decor – just the sort of place to hole up for a long, lazy winter lunch. The food tends towards the heavy, but features tasty combinations like monkfish and eggplant, and stewed rabbit with confit onions.

Valldemossa to Lluc

Xelini
Carrer Archiduque Luis Salvador 19, Deià; tel: 971 639 139; www.xelini.com; L and D, closed Mon and 10 Nov–27 Dec; €€

One of the more low-key eateries in Deià, this lively little tapas bar (previously called El Barrigon) on a pretty terrace has been going strong for many years and draws locals and visitors alike for its unfussy fare. Try the smoked ham, aubergines stuffed with goat's cheese and their speciality of *mar i muntanya* (chicken and prawns). Xelini has served many famous faces, including Catherine Zeta-Jones and Michael Douglas, Roman Polanski and Susan Sarandon.

Sa Fonda de Lluc
Plaça dels Peregrins 1, Lluc; tel: 971517 022; www.lluc.net; B, L and D; €€

This vast dining room of austere stone columns and flagstones was the pilgrims' canteen, and it has a certain monastic austerity. It's a good place for dinner at the end of a long day, to enjoy their speciality – wild mountain goat with jugs of lusty red wine. Just decide in advance who is going to drive home.

El Olivo
Carrer Son Canals s/n, Deià; tel: 971 639 011; www.belmond.com; D; €€€€

Belmond La Residencia's fine-dining restaurant draws legions of fans who can't afford a night at the hotel, but can treat themselves to a taste of the high life in elegant and refined surroundings. The modern Mallorcan tasting menu changes seasonally and is one of the best on the island. A slightly cheaper option for lunch and dinner is Café Miró, also at La Residencia, decorated with a unique collection of original paintings by the Catalan master. There is live music in the evenings.

Es Port
Port de Valldemossa s/n, Valldemossa; tel: 971 616 194; www.restaurantesport.es; L

and D; €€€

A comely restaurant spread over two floors with a pretty terrace looking back over the village and down towards the sea. The food is solid and unfussy, involving seaside classics like paella, steamed mussels, and interesting salads.

Es Racó d'es Teix

Carrer Sa Vinya Veia 6, Deià; tel: 971 639 501; http://esracodesteix.es; L and D; €€€€

Michelin-starred chefs Josef Saueschell and Leonor Payeras produce nouvelle cuisine combining the best-quality local ingredients with the highest culinary art. Portion sizes are satisfying. The *ballontine conejo* (medallions of rabbit) is delicious. Other classics include rack of lamb with olive crust, the Mediterranean fish soup and whole seabass on wild fennel for two. The food and the fairytale gardens with ravishing views make it easy to forgive the fact that it's a tad pretentious.

Sebastián

Carrer Felipe Bauzá s/n, Deià; tel: 971 639 417; Thu–Tue D, €€€

An excellent choice for a special night out if your budget doesn't quite reach the dizzying heights of El Olivo. The warm, candlelit ambience and cleverly constructed dishes, such as slow-baked lamb with honey, are just right for a romantic evening.

Sóller and Port of Sóller

Bens d'Avall

Urb Costa Deià, Ctra Sóller-Deià; tel: 971 632 381; www.bensdavall.com; opening times vary, consult the website; €€€

About half way between Sóller and Deià, this gourmet restaurant with a lovely terrace overlooking the sea specialises in New Balearic Cuisine (*nouvelle* cuisine made with local produce). Try the steamed fish with seasonal veg drizzled with herb *vinaigrette*.

Sa Cova

Plaça Constitució 7, Sóller; tel: 971 633 222; L and D; €€

Pleasant traditional restaurant with some tables on the main square. It serves good *conejo* (rabbit), which appears on many menus in the area, and seafood stew – *cazuela*. They also do a great vegetarian paella.

Lua

Carrer Santa Catalina 1, Port de Sóller; tel: 971 634 745; www.restaurantelua.es; L and D; €€

A pretty little restaurant in the Santa Caterina fishermen's district, with a more inventive take on the region's fish produce than most. Spread over two floors, the nicest place to sit is on the narrow terrace with views over the port. Enjoy tucking into local orange salad followed by a succulent fillet of John Dory slathered with *salsa verde*. Closed Mon.

El Olivo restaurant, at Belmond La Residencia

QD

Carrer Sant Ramón 1, Port de Sóller; tel: 971 632 804; www.mesquidarestaurante. com; L and D; €€

Right next to the harbour, this seafood restaurant has two terraces – upstairs and downstairs – on which to enjoy its offerings. The menu has lots of interesting salads and fish dishes, and a delicious tart made with the local Angel d'Or liqueur.

Sa Teulera

Carretera Lluc–Pollença s/n, Sóller; tel: 971 631 111; www.sateulera.es; L and D; €€

A classic for Sunday lunch, it's worth the drive (or uphill hike) from town. Roast meats cooked over almond shells are the order of the day. It gets packed to the gills, so book in advance and reserve a place on the terrace if the weather is good – it has spectacular views.

Pollença and Formentor

Clivia

Avinguda Pollentia 7, Pollença; tel: 971 533 635; L and D, closed Wed; €€

An elegant lace-curtained setting close to the main square in which to enjoy Mallorcan cuisine – fish soup, baked *lubina* (sea bass) and mountain ham are favourites.

La Font del Gall

Carrer Montesió 4, Plaça Almoina, Pollença; tel: 971 530 396; Br, L and D; €€

Owned by a Scottish family, the Font del Gall, behind Plaça Major, serves a good range of dishes in a friendly atmosphere, indoors or out on a terrace. There is a good selection of vegetarian options on the menu such as caramelised red onion and goat's cheese tart.

Il Giardino

Plaça Major 11, Pollença; tel: 971 534 302; www.giardinopollensa.com; B, L and D; €€

This family-run trattoria on the square makes a great place to sit and watch the world go by at night, when it's at its most convivial. Wood-fire cooked pizzas and home-made pastas are excellent. Next door, their shop sells French and Mallorcan cakes and chocolates. Closed Mon.

Stay

Moll Nou s/n, Port de Pollença; tel: 971 868 020/864 013; www.stayrestaurant.com; L and D; €€

A smart restaurant right in the centre of the port that has been operating for years. Fish is the first choice but there are imaginative meat dishes too, including lamb and pigeon ravioli. Caramelised walnut ice cream with green tea *coulis* is a popular dessert. Open every day of the year.

Tribeca

Carretera Formentor 43, Port de Pollença; tel 687 583 898; D, closed Sat; €€

This contemporary restaurant prides itself on having a varied menu using

fresh local ingredients. Wild mushrooms, stuffed aubergines and local trout may feature and vegetarian dishes are always available. The banoffee pancakes are delicious.

Bay of Alcúdia

Aqua

Port d'Alcúdia; tel: 971 547 833; L and D; €€

Funky Mediterranean-Asian restaurant and sushi bar with a chill-out terrace overlooking the sea. Live music and DJs Wed–Sat June–Aug. Closed Tue Apr–Oct.

Bistró de Jardín

Corner of Carrer Diana and Carrer Triton, Port d'Alcúdia; tel: 971 892 391; www.restaurantejardin.com; L and D; €€

Value-for-money Mediterranean dishes from the sister restaurant of Michelin-starred Jardín (€€€€). Try tuna *tartar* to start followed by the house hamburger and red fruit soup with yoghurt foam for dessert. There is also a gastrobar (€) here serving tapas and sandwiches.

Ca'n Costa

Carrer Sant Vinçens 14, Alcúdia; tel: 971 545 394; www.cancostaalcudia.com; L and D, closed Mon (in winter); €€€

This family-run restaurant in the oldest house in town (1594) has a lovely shady terrace out the back. Specialities include cod with garlic and honey, rabbit with onion and prawns and paellas – there's even a vegetarian one. Friendly staff and excellent service ensure a good experience. Closed mid-Jan–mid-Mar.

Casa Gallega

Hostalería 11, Port de Alcúdia; tel: 971-545 179; www.casagallegaalcudia.com; L and D; €€

Modern rustic tapas bar with an excellent selection of mouth-watering dishes from Galicia at value-for-money prices. Try the grilled squid with garlic and parsley or scrambled eggs with seaweed and prawns. They even offer a free 'tapa' with each drink.

Satyricon

Plaça Constitució 4, Alcúdia; tel: 971 544 997; B, L and D; €€

Housed in the grand surroundings of the old cinema in the main square, this place is perfect for romantic dinners and people watching, especially if you are seated on the balcony. The décor recalls Ancient Rome but the food is decidedly modern market cuisine. Desserts include flambéed strawberries with Amaretto and pineapple soup with spices and coconut cream.

Trattoria Don Vito

Carretera Alcúdia–Artà 11, Port d'Alcúdia; tel: 971 548 074; www.don-vito.com; L and D; €€

A handy standby for pizza and pasta at the end of the day, offering a solid range of Italian classics as well as more

Work up an appetite walking the castle walls

sophisticated dishes such as *vitello ton-nato* and *osso buco*.

Artà and Cala Torta

Finca Es Serral

Carretera Cala Torta Km 5, Artà; tel: 971 835 336; fincaesserral.com/Restaurante-Es-Serral; L and D, closed Mon; €€

It's a delight to know that restaurants like this still exist: Es Serral is the very heart and soul of a true farm restaurant. All the fruit and vegetables are grown on the owner's plot, the meat reared locally and the food home-cooked. Reserve well in advance to secure a table (and opening hours can be erratic, especially out of season), but it is well worth the forward planning. Closed Nov–Mar.

La Fragua

Carrer des Pla den Cosset 3, Capdepera; tel: 971 819 403; www.lafraguacapdepera.wixsite.com/lafraguacapdepera; L and D; €€

Should you make it into Capdepera, a stroll around the ancient battlements of the 14th-century castle should help you work up an appetite, which can be sated at La Fragua, which serves traditional Mallorquín dishes with an international twist on a romantic roof terrace.

Caves and Grottoes of the East

La Bodeguita

Avinguda América 14, Cala Ratjada; tel: 971 819 062; http://labodeguita.es; L and D; €

La Bodeguita does bargain-priced tapas and hearty main courses. Expect fairly basic service and food that is filling rather than award-winning, but it has pretty views over the front and is good for something cheap and cheerful. Its two sister restaurants are Taco Bar and the Green Box.

Jade

Carrer Convent 17, Alqueria Blanca Santanyí; tel: 971 653 404; D; €€€€

Finding an upmarket restaurant in the middle of a tiny little village in the back of beyond is fairly typical for Mallorca, hence the need to keep on exploring. Jade serves wonderful fusion Mediterranean cuisine in an unpretentious rural setting. Menu staples include sea bass fillet, homemade black tagliatelle with lobster and rack of lamb with tomato. Besides the excellent food, there is also an art gallery to visit.

Florian

Carrer Cristófal Colom 5, Porto Colom; tel: 971 824 171; www.restaurant-florian.com; L and D; €€€

Porto Colom has several good fish and seafood places clustered around the shore. Florian is one of the trendier ones: the chef places his cooking style firmly in the new wave, serving dishes like shellfish and fennel couscous and lobster with vanilla.

Sa Llotja

Carrer Pescadores s/n, Porto Colom;

tel: 971 825 165; www.restaurant
sallotjaportocolom.com; L and D, closed
Mon; €€€

A smart fish restaurant in the port of this
little town, Sa Llotja is raised up above
the beach on a glassed-in first floor.
It has fantastic views, which can be
especially dramatic in stormy weather
– it's open year-round – and offers a
solid repertoire of locally caught, simply cooked fish and seafood. A three-
course *menu de la semana* (weekly
menu) with wine and coffee is served
for lunch and dinner and costs €37.50
per person.

Bou Restaurant

Carrer Liles s/n, Sa Coma; tel: 971 569 663;
www.esmolidenbou.es; Sat L, Tue–Sat D;
€€€€

At the Sa Coma Playa Hotel & Spa,
Tomeu Caldentey's creative New
Mallorcan Cuisine has earned him a
Michelin star. In 2015 the restaurant
changed its name from Es Moli d'En
Bou to Bou Restaurant and a new
culinary concept was introduced. The
old classics such as venison with red
fruits or pistachio are still offered in
special 'classics' menus served on
Wednesdays (dinner) and Saturdays
(lunch).

Es Trenc and the South

Asador Es Teatre

Plaça San Bartolomé 4, Ses Salines; tel:
971 649 540; www.asadoresteatre.com; L
and D; €€

One of the trendiest restaurants in the
south, this atmospheric Argentinian
steak house covers two floors (one of
them a wrap-around gallery) and specialises in *criollo*-style barbecue (where
the meat is spatch-cocked and placed
around the flame as opposed to on it).

Es Coc

Carrer Aljub 37, Santanyí; tel: 971 641 631;
www.restaurantescoc.com; L and D, closed
Sun; €€

In the centre of town, in an old house
decorated in minimalist style, local chef
Marc Vidal serves up his interpreta-
tions of traditional Mallorcan cuisine.
There are various set menus to choose
from including a €35 degustation menu
including gazpacho soup, sepia and
avocado salad and cannelloni curry.
They do cocktails too.

Restaurant Es Port

Carrer Virgen del Carmen 88, Cala Figuera;
tel: 971 165 140; L and D; €€

A jolly, family-run place that's big on
crowd-pleasing classics ranging from
tapas and sangria, grilled fish and
man-sized steaks, stuffed aubergines
and grilled vegetable salads, through
to home-made pizza and pasta. It's
a sweet location, too, with wonderful
views over the port. Booking is essential.

Sal de Coco

Moll de Pescadors, Colonia de
Sant Jordi; tel: 971 655 225;
www.restaurantsaldecoco.com; L and D,

Petra is a great spot for foodies

closed Mon; €€€

Run by a young female chef and her sisters, this modern restaurant is named after the local salt. House specials include fish from La Cabrera, home-made pastas such as spinach and prawn ravioli with curry sauce and Idiazabal cheese with quince for dessert. There is a good wine list too.

Felanitx to Petra

Es Brot

Carrer Ràpita 44, Campos; tel: 653 751 528; Tue–Sun L and Tue–Sat D; €€€

Often described as the best traditional restaurant in Mallorca, Es Brot's diverse menu of classics like pork-stuffed cabbage leaves, pickled partridge and sturdy rice dishes is excellent. Be sure to come with a healthy appetite.

Es Celler

Carrer de l'Hospital 46, Petra; tel: 971 561 056; L and D, closed Mon; €€

Huge and cavernous restaurant serving heaped plates of traditional food, including meat roasted in a traditional wood oven.

Son Bascos

Carretera Palma-Manacor, Km 29, Montuiri; tel: 971 646 170; L and D, closed Tue; €

Set on a quail farm, the speciality of this traditional Mallorcan restaurant is, of course, quail. Try quails' eggs with garlic mayonnaise to start followed by grilled quail with salad. Don't panic if you don't fancy quail – there

are other dishes on offer, including options for vegetarians. The home-made desserts include carrot and almond cake.

Wine Country

Celler Can Amer

Carrer Pau 39, Inca; tel: 971 501 261; www.celler-canamer.es; L and D; €€

Opened in 1700, the barrels, copper pots and flagstone floors make this a wonderfully atmospheric place for long, boozy lunches (particularly in the winter). Chef Antonia Cantallops combines the Jewish, Arabic and Christian influences of the island's culinary heritage to create her variation on traditional cuisine, but it's always superb. The shoulder of lamb stuffed with aubergines and *sobrasada* is awe-inspiring. Closed Sat and Sun from May–Sept.

Celler Can Ripoll

Carrer Jaume Armengol 4, Inca; tel: 971 500 024; www.restaurantcanripoll.com; B, Br, L and D, closed Sun evening; €€

Opened in 1768, this cellar restaurant was, like Can Amer, used mainly by local workers as a place to fill their wine jugs. Food wasn't offered until the 1940s, the speciality being a fairly hardcore *frito mallorquín* – stir-fried offal. These days you can also find excellent but rather more pedestrian stuffed cabbage leaves and roast suckling pig. The daily menu (weekdays only) is a real bargain at €10.95.

NIGHTLIFE

If you're looking for frenetic nightlife, Mallorca probably isn't the island for you, although things can get lively in Palma in the summer. Once outside the city you will find a much slower pace of life, especially when you hit rural areas and some of the quieter coastal towns and villages. If you're staying in Estellencs (route 4), for example, the most you can hope for is a beer in the village bar, although tourist resorts tend to be livelier. For that reason, the bulk of the listings here concentrate on what's happening in Palma, with a sprinkling of recommended places elsewhere.

Palma

Ábaco

Carrer Sant Joan 1; tel: 971 714 939; www.bar-abaco.es
No visit to Palma is complete without stopping at this legendary cocktail bar. Famed for its over-the-top decor, and gigantic fruit and floral arrangements, there's nowhere quite like it for your gin and tonic.

Auditorium

Passeig Marítim 18; tel: 971 735 328; http://auditoriumpalma.com
Home to the Ciutat de Palma Symphony Orchestra and a host of cultural events throughout the year, ranging from contemporary dance to opera. Check out what's on ahead of your trip; tickets can be hard to come by.

Casino de Mallorca

Porto Pi Centro; tel: 971 130 000; open until 5am; www.casinodemallorca.com
The island's only casino can be fun. It's a fairly upmarket place once you get away from the slot machines, and provides a good excuse to get dressed up and indulge in an *Ocean's Eleven*-style fantasy.

Cine Ciutat

Carrer Emperatrix Eugenia 6; tel: 971 205 453; www.cineciutat.org
The only original-language cinema in town, Cine Ciutat, formerly Cine Renoir, shows a fair number of independent films as well as the blockbusters. Auditoriums are small and cosy, giving it an art-house feel.

Cuba Bar and Restaurant

Carrer de Sant Magí 1, Palma Centre & Marina; tel: 971 452 237
Housed in a beautiful colonial building in the trendy Santa Catalina district of Palma, this popular café, bar and club features wicker chairs and leafy palms in the ground floor café and a rooftop Sky Bar offering great sunset views over Palma. There is also a restaurant serving Mediterranean dishes. Downstairs is where the DJ's spin their

Mallorca has plenty of options for when the sun goes down

tunes until the small hours. Open daily until 2am.

Jazz Voyeur Club
Carrer Apuntadors 5; tel: 971 720 780; www.jazzvoyeur.com
Formerly the Barcelona Jazz Club, this was one of the city's first live music venues, and dedicates itself mainly to live jazz and blues, with the odd jam session for good measure.

Made in Brasil
Passeig Marítim 27; tel: 670 372 390
If you seek samba, salsa and other snake-hipped Latin rhythms, this is where to head; the place sizzles until 4am most nights of the week, attracting some serious dancers.

Puro Beach
Cala Estancia s/n (airport exit); tel: 971 744 744; www.purobeach.com
The first of a growing number of swanky beach clubs to pepper the coast, Puro is the full-time haunt of the island's beautiful crowd in summer. It opens early for sunbathing by the pool, yoga sessions and champagne brunches, segueing effortlessly into a more clubby vibe once the sun goes down.

Tito's
Passeig Marítim s/n; tel: 971 730 017; www.titosmallorca.com
Tito's attracts a slightly more grown-up crowd than other clubs along the disco mile and is the longest-standing club on the island. It has a certain old-school appeal with an exterior glass lift and laser light show, spectacular views of the port by night and a strong repertoire of favourite club anthems.

Virtual Club
Passeig Illetes 60, Illetes; tel: 971 703 235; www.virtualclub.es
Mallorca's second beach club – after Puro – Virtual is a little less achingly trendy and offers a more relaxed vibe. Like Puro, you can spend the day lounging by the sea, have lunch, then let your sundowner lead you gently into the evening.

Nikki Beach
Avinguda Notario Alemany 1, Magaluf; tel: 971 123 962; www.nikkibeach.com
One of the latest offerings from the chain of exclusive beach clubs with branches in St Tropez and St Barts. Rent a sunbed by day and party at night – if you think you are young, rich and cool enough. Closed in winter.

Pirates
Carretera Sa Porrassa 12, Magaluf; tel: 971 130 411; www.piratesadventure.com
The show at Pirates has been running since the early 1980s and is wildly popular. Book well in advance and treat the whole family to what may be the best '*espectaculo*' this side of Broadway.

Flying the EU flag

A–Z

A

Age restrictions

As of 2015 the age of consent in Spain is 16 for both heterosexual and homosexual sex. You can smoke and drink from 18. To drive a car or motorbike over 125cc you need to be over 18.

B

Budgeting

Mallorca has become more expensive in recent years due to the fluctuating euro rate and the island increasingly becoming an upmarket destination. All prices below are approximate and given only as a guide.

Getting there

Air fares vary enormously. Flights from the UK with a budget airline can vary from around £60 return in off-season to £190 or more in high season. Scheduled flights can be as low as £130 if you book well in advance, but anything up to £300 if you make a relatively late booking. The cheapest flights are usually available via the internet, or by taking a chance on a last-minute offer. Check out the website www.skyscanner.net to compare prices.

Accommodation

Hotels can be more expensive than on the Spanish mainland. Rates for two sharing a double room during high season can range from as low as €45 in a *hostal* to as much as €400 at a top-of-the-range hotel. A comfortable, pleasant three-star hotel will cost about €80–€120. Rates drop considerably out of season.

Meals

The *menú del día*, a fixed price midday meal, is usually an excellent bargain, costing around €12–15 for a reasonably good three-course meal with one drink included. In a bar a continental breakfast (fresh orange juice, coffee and croissant) will cost around €5; a coffee €1.50–€2. The average price of a three-course à la carte meal, including house wine, will be about €35 per person. You can pay considerably less, but at top restaurants you may pay more than twice that much. The price of wine has increased: you will pay about €2.50–€3 for a glass of wine in a smartish bar.

Attractions

Most museums and galleries charge an entry fee of around €3–5. Entry to La Real Cartuja, Valldemossa costs €8.50; the Coves del Drach around €15. Water parks are more expensive, around €25

Parc del Mar, Palma   *Numerous beaches are safe for children*

(children €18). A two-hour trip in a glass-bottomed boat costs around €15 (children half-price).

Ferries

Inter-island ferries between Mallorca and Menorca are reasonable for foot passengers (about €50 return), but quite expensive if you take a car – about €200 for a vehicle and two passengers. The ferry from Mallorca to Ibiza is about the same price. Deals are often available, especially if you book well in advance.

Useful prices

A *caña* (small draught beer): €2.00
Glass of house wine: €2–4
Main course: budget restaurant €7.90, mid-range €15, expensive €21+
Hotels: budget €45, moderate €80, luxury €200+
Taxi from Palma airport to city centre: €27
A single bus ticket: €1.50

C

Children

The Spanish adore kids. Even fairly late at night, you will find that restaurants welcome little ones with open arms, and most serve child-friendly meals. Nearly all sights and theme parks offer a discount for under-12s, and resort hotels are generally pretty good when it comes to children's activities.

Climate

Mid-June until September is virtually rainless, with wall-to-wall sunshine. In July, the hottest month, temperatures range from 30°C (86°F) in the afternoon to about 20°C (68°F) at night. Autumn temperatures are typically around 24°C (75°F), but there are often short heavy rains in early September; October is the wettest month. April and May see a little rain with lots of sunshine and moderate temperatures. In winter, expect some rain and cool winds, but most days are sunny, and it is usually warm enough at midday to sit outside. Average maximum/minimum winter temperatures are 15°C (59°F) and 7°C (45°F).

Clothing

Mallorca is pretty low-key, though older people dress up a bit for their evening *paseo* (promenade); a T-shirt and shorts are the minimum requirement for both men and women. Never wear beach gear in towns (you can now be fined for this), and when visiting churches cover your shoulders and knees. Going topless on the beaches is fairly normal, though total nudity should be kept to designated beaches.

In spring and autumn bring lots of light layers and a mac. In summer you won't need much more than something to cover up with, but bring something warm and waterproof in the winter.

Pristine paintwork in Fornalutz

Crime and safety

Mallorca is generally pretty safe and serious crime extremely rare. Employ the same precautions you would anywhere, though: keep your eye on belongings, especially in crowded areas, and take care when withdrawing money from ATMs. Leave extra valuables in the hotel safe; make a photocopy of your passport and carry it with you. If you hire a car, don't leave property visible inside.

If any of your property is lost or stolen you must report it to the police within 24 hours if you intend to make a claim on your insurance policy.

Customs

EU nationals may purchase up to 800 cigarettes, 200 cigars or 1kg tobacco, 10l of spirits and 90l of wine. Non-EU nationals may purchase 200 cigarettes, 50 cigars, 250g loose tobacco, 1l spirits and 2l wine.

Disabled travellers

If travelling with a wheelchair, inform the airline or ferry service in advance. Help is always on hand for getting through arrival and departure halls. Not all bars, restaurants or hotels are equipped with ramps or lifts, so check the facilities in advance.

Mobility Abroad (tel: 0871 277 0888 in Spain; www.mobilityabroad. com) provides support and hire of wheelchairs and disabled-friendly vehicles throughout the Balearic islands.

Electricity

220 volts AC. British appliances work perfectly well but need an adaptor, as sockets are the two round-pin type; US appliances need a transformer.

Embassies and consulates

Australia: in Madrid atTorre Espacio, Paseo de la Castellana 259D; tel: 913 536 600; www.spain.embassy.gov.au.
Canada: in Madrid at Torre Espacio, Paseo de la Castellana 259D; tel: 913 828 400; www.canadainternational. gc.ca.
Ireland: Carrer Sant Miquel 68, Palma; tel: 971 719 244; www.embassyof ireland.es.
UK: Carrer Convent dels Caputxins 4, Edificio Orisba B, Palma; tel: 902 109 356; www.gov.uk/government/world/ spain.
US: Edificio Reina Constanza, Carrer Porto Pi 8, 9th floor, Palma; tel: 971 403 707; http://madrid.usembassy. gov.

Emergencies

Police, fire, ambulance: 112
Policía Nacional: 091
Policía Municipal: 092
Guardia Civil (traffic): 062

Potential purchases in Pollença

Etiquette

Islanders are easy-going people, but be respectful of their religion, dress sensibly in towns and cities and learn a couple of words of Catalan for exchanging niceties in the street. Above all, be open – people are friendly and curious about foreign visitors.

Festivals

Most towns and villages have a local festival celebrating their patron saint, which incorporates abundant dancing, eating and drinking. The most interesting have appearances by *cavallets* – dancers with cardboard hobby-horses strapped to them – and *dimoni* – red-clad devils. Highlights include: Palma's carnival in February; Semana Santa (Holy Week) in Pollença; Moros y Cristianos (Christians and Moors) in Sóller on 8–10 May; festivals of classical music in Pollença and Deià throughout July and August; Festa des Vermar (Wine Festival) on the last Sunday of September in Binissalem. Check www.agendamallorca.net for a comprehensive list of events.

Gay and lesbian travellers

There's not a massive scene in Mallorca and most of it is concentrated in Palma, but citizens are generally gay/lesbian-friendly, and you won't encounter any problems. www.benamics.com is a good 'what's on' site, and there are quite a few lively clubs and bars in the old town. See www.mallorcagayguide.com.

Green issues

Mallorca has invested heavily in developing 'slow tourism' by expanding hiking trails, bicycle routes and *agroturismos* (rural hotels and restaurants) which often grow their own produce. The tourist 'eco tax' introduced in 2016 aims to promote responsible development and tourism.

Health

Inoculations
None required.

Health care and insurance
EU citizens are eligible for free treatment in state-run hospitals. UK visitors should obtain a European Health Insurance Card (EHIC) from a post office or online (www.ehic.org.uk). Visitors from the US will need private health insurance, and it is strongly advised that all travellers take out medical and travel insurance.

Pharmacies and hospitals
Major hospitals and clinics in Palma include: **Centro Médico**, Edificio

Reina Constanza, Passeig Marítim (Porto Pi) 8; tel: 971 707 035; www.centromedicoportopi.es (many of the staff speak English); and for accidents and emergencies Son Espases, Carretera de Valldemossa; tel: 871 205 000, where some staff also speak English and German.

Most towns and villages have first-aid stations or doctor's surgeries: the *Casa de Socorro* or *Cruz (Creu) Roja*. There are pharmacies *(farmacias)* on most main streets in Palma (look out for the green cross), and in all major towns. In most towns an effective system of rotation operates whereby there is always one chemist open round-the-clock in each area. A sign in front of each should indicate which chemists are on duty that night, and which is closest to where you are. Some pharmacies, such as Farmacia Balanguera (www.farmaciabalanguera.com), are open 24 hours. *Farmacias* are amply stocked with over-the-counter remedies, and many drugs can be purchased without prescription; however, your particular medication may not be available, and they do not honour foreign prescriptions, so bring with you any prescription medicine you require.

Medical emergencies

If you have a medical emergency while in Spain, your hotel should be able to recommend reliable professionals who speak several languages. The local embassy or consulate will also have a list of English-speaking doctors. You can also go to the local hospital emergency department or medical clinic to receive treatment on presentation of a European Health Insurance Card. If no help is near at hand, call the medical emergency number: 061.

Hours and holidays

Hours still revolve around the long lunch-time siesta, though that is slowly changing. Shop hours are 9.30am–1.30pm and 4.30–8pm. Museums are open 9am–6pm (although smaller ones may keep the siesta).

Banks are only open in the mornings from 9.30am–2pm, Monday to Friday, but some open on Saturday in winter. Restaurants serve lunch from 1.30–3.30pm. In the evening local people usually eat between 9.30 and 11pm.

Internet

Since 2014 practically the whole of Palma is covered with free Wi-fi. The island's authorities plan to extend the free coverage beyond the city limits, but the process is a lengthy one and there are still many areas without a reliable Wi-fi connection. You can check the list of free and paid hotspots outside Palma (and on the other Balearic islands) at www.islawifi.com.

Admiring the view from Castell de Bellver, outside Palma

L

Lost property

There are lost property departments at the airport on the ground floor (tel: 971 789 456) and at Palma's Town Hall. It is also worth checking with the police station nearest to where you lost your belongings.

M

Maps

Free tourist maps of Palma are given out at most hotels and the tourist office, likewise in bigger towns like Sóller. In rural areas maps are useful for getting your bearings, but not very reliable for route planning.

Media

Print media

Most UK and German papers arrive daily in Palma and the main resorts, along with the *International Herald Tribune*, *Wall Street Journal* and *USA Today*. The English-language *Majorca Daily Bulletin* (http://majorcadaily bulletin.com) gives local and UK news and entertainment listings. Local publications the *Diario de Mallorca* (www. diariodemallorca.es) and *Guía del Ocio* (www.guiadelocio.com/illes-balears) are good for up-to-the-minute information on what's on, and all the Spanish national newspapers and magazines are widely available.

Television

Most hotels and bars have television, broadcasting in Castilian, Catalan and Mallorquí. All but the smallest of hotels generally have satellite channels (predominantly German, but also French, channels along with the ubiquitous English-language Sky, BBC, CNN, etc.).

Money

Currency

The euro has been the Spanish monetary unit since 2002.

Credit cards

Major international credit cards Visa, Eurocard and MasterCard are widely accepted, but smaller businesses tend to prefer cash. American Express is only accepted in some places.

Cash machines

Credit and debit cards are useful for obtaining cash from ATMs – cash machines – found in all towns and resorts; they usually offer the best exchange rate, though many banks charge commission. Many travel agencies exchange foreign currency, and *casas de cambio* stay open outside banking hours.

Tipping

In some restaurants service is already included (look for *servicio incluído* on the bill). Otherwise, tips range from rounding up to the nearest euro at a bar, to 10 percent in a smart restaurant.

Botanicactus botanical garden

Taxes

Spain applies a standard rate of VAT (IVA) of 21 percent on most goods and services, including hotels; 10 percent is charged on foodstuffs and in restaurants. The 2016 tourist tax adds up to €2 to the daily rate of accommodation.

Reclaiming VAT

In order to be eligible, as a tourist, for a refund of the Spanish IVA (Value Added Tax), you must come from a non-EU country and spend €90.16 or more in a single shop. Tell the shop that you intend to reclaim the VAT, which is currently 21 percent in Spain. You will be given a form which you must get stamped at a duty reduction office at the airport before departure. Go to the desk of one of the companies authorised to give you a tax refund. If you leave the country other than by air, get the customs post to validate your form and then take a copy back to the shop you bought the goods from and it will make the refund. The process is explained at www.globalblue.com.

Police

In an emergency dial 112.

There are three types of police, distinguishable by their uniforms: in black and white are the Policía Nacional, who are in charge of most things. The Policía Municipal (Local or Metropolitan) are responsible for traffic control, while the Guardia Civil, still dressed in traditional dark-green uniforms, have jurisdiction only in rural areas.

Post

Palma's main post office is at Carrer Constitució 6 and is open Monday to Friday 8.30am–8.30pm, Saturday 9.30am–1pm. Other post offices on the island (all recognisable by a yellow and white sign and the words *Correos y Telégrafos*) are only open 8.30am–2.30pm. Post boxes are yellow.

Stamps can also be bought at tobacconists *(estancos)*, which are easily identifiable by their maroon and yellow *Tabacos* sign over the door. A postcard or letter to countries in Europe currently costs €1.15; to the US €1.30).

Public holidays

As in all Catholic countries, local saints' days may be celebrated as holidays, but only the days of the major saints (see the list below) are public holidays throughout the island.

1 Jan: New Year's Day (Año Nuevo/Any Nou)

6 Jan: Epiphany (Reyes Magos/Reis Mags)

19 Mar: St Joseph (San José/Sant Josep)

Good Friday (Viernes Santo/Divendres Sant)

1 May: Labour Day (Dia del Trabajo/Treball)

Ninth Thursday after Easter: Corpus Christi

Cala Mesquida — *Sunset over the coast*

24 June: St John (San Juan/Sant Joan)
29 June: St Peter and Paul (San Pedro y San Pablo/Sant Pere i Sant Pau)
25 July: St James (Santiago/Sant Jaume)
15 Aug: Day of the Assumption (Asunción/Assumpció)
12 Oct: Spanish National Day (Dia de la Hispanidad/Hispanitat)
1 Nov: All Saints (Todos los Santos/Tots Sants)
6 Dec: Constitution Day (Dia de la Constitución/Constitució)
8 Dec: Immaculate Conception (Inmaculada Concepión/Concepció)
Christmas Day (Navidad/Nadal)

R

Religion

The official religion of Mallorca is Catholicism, though the majority of locals are fairly lax about it. Many attend mass at Christmas and Easter, when it can be quite festive.

S

Smoking

As of 1 January 2011 smoking has been banned in public places across Spain.

T

Telephones

Public telephones

Public telephone booths are becoming increasingly rare as more and more people have mobile phones. However, you can make direct-dial local and international calls from those that still exist. Many only operate with a phone card *(tarjeta telefónica)*, which can be purchased at any *estanco* (tobacconist's), but others also accept coins. International telephone credit cards can also be used. Instructions for use are given in several languages in the booths.

You can also make calls at public telephone offices called *locutorios* – much quieter than making a call on the street, and generally cheaper. These telephone offices are identified by a blue and white sign. An attendant will place the call for you, and you pay afterwards.

International calls

To make an international call, dial 00 for an international line plus the country code plus the phone number, omitting any initial zero. Calls are cheaper after 10pm on weekdays, after 2pm on Saturday, and all day Sunday.

The international code for Spain is 34. To call within Spain, you must always dial the area code (971 for the Balearics), then the number, even when phoning within the same town.

Mobile (cell) phones

Most UK mobile phones can be used in the Balearics. Contact your service provider if you are unsure, and it's a good idea to find out about any money-saving tips such as buying bundles of min-

Quad bikes for hire in Magaluf

utes. It is cheaper to receive calls than to make them.

If you are going to make lots of calls within Spain it is worth buying a Spanish SIM card or new phone from a phone shop. Well-known networks are Movistar (www.movistar.es), Orange (www.orange.es) and Vodafone (www.vodafone.es).

Time zone

Spain is on Central European Time, one hour ahead of Greenwich Mean Time. When it is noon in London, it is 1pm in Mallorca.

Toilets

Toilets *(serveis/servicios)* are generally clean and well kept, but public toilets are few and far between. If you duck into a bar you should buy something, as most are for patrons only. In Palma, head for a department store such as El Corte Inglés. *Dones/damas* stands for ladies, *cavallers/caballeros* for gentlemen.

Tourist information

Tourist information is readily available in most parts of Mallorca, although many offices close in winter. The following list is not comprehensive.

Local tourist offices
Palma: Plaça de la Reina 2, tel: 971173 990; Passeig del Born 27, tel: 902 102 365; Plaça de Espanya, tel: 902 102 365; Parc de la Mar, tel: 902 102 365; Plaça de les Meravelles, Platja de Palma, tel: 902 102 365.
Airport: tel: 971 789 556.
Alcúdia: Passeig Pere Ventanyol s/n, tel: 971 549 022, www.alcudiamallorca.com.
Colònia Sant Jordi: Gabriel Roca s/n, tel: 971 656 073 (closed Nov–Mar), www.ajsessalines.net.
Pollença: Guillem Cifre de Colonya s/n, tel: 971 535 077, www.pollensa.com.
Port d'Alcúdia: Passeig Maritím s/n, tel: 971 547 257 (closed Nov–Mar), www.alcudiamallorca.com.
Port de Pollença: Passeig Saralegui s/n, tel: 971 865 467, www.pollensa.com.
Port de Sóller: Canonge Oliver 10, tel: 971 633 042 (closed Nov–Mar), www.soller.es.
Sóller: Plaça d'Espanya 15, tel: 971 638 008, www.soller.es.
Valldemossa: Avinguda de Palma 7, tel: 971 612 019 (closed Nov–Mar), www.valldemossa.es.

Tourist offices abroad
Canada: 2 Bloor Street West, Suite 3402, Toronto, Ontario M4W 3E2, tel: 416-961 3131, www.spain.info/en_CA.
UK: 64 North Row, London W1K 7DE, tel: 020 7317 2011; www.spain.info/en_GB.
US: Water Tower Place, Suite 915 East, 845 North Michigan Avenue, Chicago, IL 60611, tel: 312-642 1992; 8383; Wilshire Boulevard, Suite 960, Beverly Hills, CA 90211, tel: 213-658 7188;

Cycle route along the seafront

Suite 5300, 60 East 42nd Street, New York, NY 10165–0039, tel: 212-265 8822; Suite 1130, 1395 Brickell Avenue, Miami, FL 33131, tel: 305-358 1992; www.spain.info/en_US.

Tours

Local tourist offices will have details of guided bus and walking tours in the area but here is a selection of more interesting ones:

Cooltra: Carrer Monsenyor Palmer 3, Palma, www.cooltra.com. Small group tours around Palma by scooter.

Mallorca Hiking: tel: 07979 656 332 (UK), www.mallorcahiking.com. A wide range of guided walks for all levels including strenuous hikes, gastronomy and architecture.

Mallorca Wine Tours: tel: 653 528 659, www.mallorcawinetours.com. Tours of Mallorca's vineyards on a small tourist train.

Palma City Sightseeing: tel: 902 101 081, www.city-ss.es/es/palma-de-mallorca. Open-top bus tours of Palma.

Tramuntana Tours: tel: 971 632 423, www.tramuntanatours.com. Walking, mountain biking and sea-kayaking in small groups.

Transport

Airports and arrival

Palma de Mallorca's huge **Son Sant Joan airport** (PMI; www.aena.es) is linked by regular scheduled non-stop flights from London, Dublin, Berlin and Frankfurt, with frequent flights from many other European cities. Flights from the US and Canada also go via London airports and Barcelona or Madrid. Numerous budget airlines fly to Palma from airports all over the UK. Booking via the internet is usually cheapest for flight-only tickets.

The airport is about 11km (7 miles) from the city centre. There are buses every 20 minutes (journey time about 30 minutes). Bus No. 1 operates from 6am to 1.10am (1.50am in summer) and runs to Plaça d'Espanya, and to the port with stops en route (€3).Taxis are readily available (journey time about 15–20 minutes) and fares are reasonable.

Arriving by boat

Car ferries operate daily from Barcelona and Valencia to Palma. The slower, overnight trip takes 8 hours on Trasmediterránea (Moll de Paraires, Estació Marítim 2; tel: 902 454 645 or 971 702 300/971 366 050 in Palma; www.trasmediterranea.es); during peak holiday season, it also operates a faster ferry, which takes 4.5 hours. Baleària operates a fast ferry from Barcelona to Alcúdia on Saturday and Sunday, which takes 5.5 hours (tel: 902 160 180; www.balearia.net).

Public transport

Buses

There are several bus companies in Mallorca, travelling to virtually every point on the island. In Palma, most ser-

Marina at Andratx

vices begin at the Plaça de Espanya or the bus station close by in Carrer Eusebio Estada (near the railway station) – see www.tib.org for details. City buses are also efficient. There is a set fare for city journeys, and you buy your ticket on the bus. A Palma bus schedule detailing city routes from Empresa Municipal de Transports (EMT) is available from the tourist office or see www.emtpalma.es.

Metro

Palma's metro system is the fifth in Spain and consists of two lines (M1, M2) with nine stations each. M1 connects Estación Intermodal on Plaza de España with the university, while M2 links Plaza de España with Marratxí.

Trains

As well as the famous old train, which runs seven times a day (five in winter) between Palma and Sóller, there is a train from Palma's Plaça de Espanya to Inca which runs on to Sa Pobla and Manacor. Primarily a commuter train, it leaves both the island capital and Inca about once every hour, with extra trains at rush hour, stopping at Santa Maria del Camí, Consell and Binissalem along the way. For Sóller trains (www.trende soller.com), tel: 971 752 051; for Inca and Manacor trains, tel: 971177 777, see www.tib.org or ask at the station.

Taxis

Palma has several taxi ranks, and cabs can be hailed on the street. All have meters and are reasonably priced, though you pay extra for luggage and trips to and from the airport. Trips across the island, however, are quite expensive. Official prices are posted at cab ranks, and drivers also carry a list.

Driving in Mallorca

Rules and regulations

Drive on the right. Seat belts are compulsory for front and back seats. Children under 12 must be seated in a booster seat. Don't drink and drive: the permitted blood-alcohol level is low and penalties are strict. Compulsory equipment includes a spare tyre, a warning triangle and a reflective jacket.

Road conditions

Generally good, although many are narrow, and mountain routes have numerous hairpin bends and can get very busy in the summer. The motorway that loops around to the north of Palma (connecting the airport with points west of the city), is known as the *Via Cintura* and is signposted as such.

Speed limits

Motorways 120kmph (74mph), two-lane highways 100kmph (62mph), other main roads 90kmph (55mph), built-up areas 50kmph (31mph), unless otherwise indicated.

Parking

In Palma this can be difficult. Your best bet is to head for one of the city centre underground car parks (for instance at Plaça Mayor or opposite the cathedral at the Parc de la Mar). Parking fines are steep, and as it is more difficult to collect fines from tourists, there is a tendency to tow away hire cars.

Hiring a car is the easiest way to explore the island

Car hire

This is relatively inexpensive, and all the major international agencies are represented, along with some local agents that are generally cheaper. In high season, book well in advance and remember that local companies often set a minimum rental of three or four days. Always check what's included: third-party insurance is, by law, but fully comprehensive is usually extra and it is advisable to have it. You need to be 21 to hire a car and must have a full driving licence and a credit card.

Bicycle and scooter hire

A practical and enjoyable way to see the island is to hire a bicycle, and this can be done in most resorts – hotels and tourist offices have leaflets. Mopeds and scooters are also available, but you'll need a special licence. Prices vary widely, so shop around. Remember that a helmet is compulsory when riding a motorcycle, whatever the engine size. Ask for a helmet and for a pump and puncture kit, in case you get stuck with a flat tyre, and always carry ID. In Palma, go to Palma on bike, Avinguda Gabriel Roca 15, tel: 971 918 988, www.palmaonbike.com. Pro Cycle Hire will deliver your bike direct to your resort hotel if arranged in advance; tel: 971 866 857 or check www.procyclehire.com. It also organises daily ride-outs at 9am (meeting point in front of the shop at Carrer Corb Mari 6, Puerto Pollença).

Visas and passports

British citizens just need a valid passport. Visitors from other EU countries require a valid national identity card. US citizens, Australians and New Zealanders require a valid passport and are automatically authorised for a three-month stay.

Websites

Useful websites are peppered throughout the book, but the following are good for general information:
www.seemallorca.com: for tips on what's on and where to go.
www.mallorca.co.uk: for villa rentals.
www.illesbalears.travel or www.infomallorca.net: the official tourism portals for the island.
www.digamemallorca.com: good general information.
www.palma.cat: Palma city council's site.
www.angloinfo.com/balearics: business directory, classifieds and what's on.

Weights and measures

Mallorca uses the metric system.

Women travellers

Women travelling alone will find Mallorca an easy-going, non-threatening place to explore. As anywhere, avoid walking home late at night alone.

Sample Mallorca's signature pastries

LANGUAGE

Mallorca's language is Mallorquí, a dialect of Catalan. During Franco's dictatorship the teaching and publication of Catalan was banned, and replaced by Spanish/Castilian (Castellano), although people still spoke the language at home. With the arrival of regional autonomy in 1978, Catalan/Mallorquí was re-established, and has become a symbol of Mallorcan identity, although everyone also speaks Spanish.

As a result of this, maps and street signs use Castilian or Catalan at random. Most words are fairly similar, but some are completely unrelated. Signs indicating various points of touristic or other interest are almost always in Catalan. Throughout this book, we have tried to give the Catalan version of the place name and the words and phrases below are also in the official local parlance.

Useful words and phrases

General
yes *sí*
no *no*
please *si us plau*
thank you (very much) *(moltes) gràcies*
you're welcome *de res*
excuse me *perdoni*
hello *hola*
good morning *bon dia*
good afternoon *bona tarda*
good evening/night *bona nit*
goodbye *adéu*
How much is it? *Quant val?*
What is your name? *Com es diu?*
OK *d'acord*
My name is… *Em dic…*
Do you speak English? *Parla anglès?*
I am English/American *Sóc anglès (anglesa)/americà/ana*
I don't understand *No ho entenc*
Please speak more slowly *Parli més a poc a poc, sisplau*
Can you help me? *Em pot ajudar?*
I'm looking for… *Estic buscant…*
Where is…? *On és…?*
I'm sorry *Ho sento*
I don't know *No ho sé*
When? *Quan?*
What time is it? *Quina hora és?*
left *esquerra*
right *dreta*
straight on *tot recte*
opposite *al davant*
beside *al costat*

On arrival
I want to get off at… *Voldria baixar a…*
Is there a bus to…? *Hi ha un autobús cap a…?*
Which line do I take for…? *Quina línia agafo per…?*
airport *l'aeroport*
railway station *l'estació de tren*
bus station *l'estació d'autobusos*
bus *l'autobús*
platform *l'andana*

Conversing in Palma, next to a headless street artist

ticket *un bitllet*
return ticket *un bitllet de anada i tornada*
toilets *els lavabos/serveis*

Emergencies
Help! *Auxili!*
Stop! *Pari!*
I am sick *Em trobo malament*
I have lost my passport/wallet *He perdut el passaport/la cartera*

Shopping
I'd like to buy… *Voldria comprar…*
How much is it? *Quant val?*
Do you take credit cards? *Es pot pagar amb targeta?*
I'm just looking *Estic mirant*
receipt *el tiquet*
chemist *la farmàcia*
bakery *el forn de pa*
book shop *la llibreria*
department store *els grans magatzems*
grocery *el botiga de queviures*
tobacconist *l'estanc*
market *el mercat*
supermarket *el supermercat*

Sightseeing
tourist information office *oficina de turisme*
free *gratuït*
open *obert*
closed *tancat*
every day *tots els dias*

Dining out
breakfast *l'esmorzar*

lunch *el dinar*
dinner *el sopar*
meal *el menjar*
set menu *el menú del dia*
drink included *beguda inclosa*
wine list *la carta de vins*
red wine *vi negre*
white wine *vi blanc*
the bill *el compte*
glass *la copa* (for wine), *el vas* (for water)
I am a vegetarian *Sóc vegetarià/ana*
I'd like to order *Voldria demanar*
tax included *IVA inclòs*

Days of the week
Monday *Dilluns*
Tuesday *Dimarts*
Wednesday *Dimecres*
Thursday *Dijous*
Friday *Divendres*
Saturday *Dissabte*
Sunday *Diumenge*

Social media
Are you on Facebook/Twitter? *Que tens Facebook/Twitter?*
What's your user name? *Quin és el teu nom d'usuari?*
I'll add you as a friend. *T'agregaré com a amic.*
I'll follow you on Twitter. *Et seguiré a Twitter*
Are you following…? *Segueixes…?*
I'll put the pictures on Facebook/Twitter. *Penjaré les fotos a Facebook/Twitter.*
I'll tag you in the pictures. *T'etiquetaré a les fotos.*

Library at Real Cartuja (Royal Carthusain monastery) de Valldemossa

BOOKS AND FILM

Until fairly recently, Mallorca has been largely ignored by the worlds of literature and film. However, little by little over the past decade, humorous expat memoirs à la Peter Mayle and Chris Stewart have been inching out and the island is increasingly used as a film location – multi-million pound investments have created two state-of-the-art studios.

Here is a selection of the best English-language books and movies. For further information about local books visit Fine Books, Carrer Morey 7, Palma and for the latest film news see www.imdb.com.

Books

General background
Mallorca: The Making of the Landscape by Richard Buswell. An interesting read about the island's history.
Tuning up at Dawn by Tomàs Graves. Robert Graves's son writes about life and music.
Wild Olives by William Graves. Robert Graves's other son's account of growing up in Deià.

Walking, climbing and birdwatching
Finding Birds in Mallorca by Dave Gosney. Shows the best sites to see Mallorca's birdlife.
Walking in Mallorca by June Parker. Detail of more than 70 hikes all over the island.

Landscapes of Mallorca byValerie Crespi-Green. A perfect companion for walkers and hikers.

Food
The Taste of a Place: Mallorca by Vicky Bennison. A mouth-watering introduction to Mallorcan food.
Bread and Oil by Tomàs Graves. An insider's look at two of Mallorca's great products.

Travel accounts
Snowball Oranges by Peter Kerr. The first of several entertaining books about a Scottish expat settling into life on the island.
A Lizard in my Luggage by Anna Nicholas. The first of several enjoyable books

Frédéric Chopin and George Sand lived at the monastery

by a London PR consultant who moves to the Sóller Valley.

A Winter in Majorca by George Sand. Sand's scathing account of her stay on the island in 1838–9 with Chopin (translated by Robert Graves).

A House in the High Hills: Dreams and Disasters of Life in a Spanish Farmhouse by Selina Scott. The former TV newsreader's humorous account of renovating her property in the Serra de Tramuntana.

Fiction

The Bloody Bokhara by George Scott. Mallorcan murder mystery set in the now-closed Scott's Hotel in Binissalem.

Murdered by Nature by Roderic Jefferies. The latest in a series of murder mysteries investigated by Inspector Alvarez.

The Mallorca Connection by Peter Kerr. The first of several comedic crime novels featuring fictional Scottish detective Bob Burns.

Rafael's Wings by Sian Mackay. A Scottish ornithologist finds herself in a mysterious world when she goes to work in the Mallorcan mountains.

Film and TV

Our Girl Friday (1953). British comedy starring Joan Collins about a woman who is shipwrecked on a desert island with three men.

The 7th Voyage of Sinbad (1958). Some of the scenes from this much-loved fantasy film with special effects by Ray Harryhausen were shot in the Coves d'Artà.

Evil Under the Sun (1982). Several locations in Mallorca including Sa Dragonera and Formentor were used for this star-studded interpretation of Agatha Christie's book.

Presence of Mind (1999). Filmed on the Raixa Estate and starring Harvey Keitel and Sadie Frost, this film is a chilling adaptation of **The Turn of the Screw** by Henry James.

Four Last Songs (2006). *Downton Abbey*'s Hugh Bonneville leads an international cast in this British romantic comedy with a musical theme.

Cloud Atlas (2013). Sa Calobra, Sóller and Formentor are the real stars of this adaptation of David Mitchell's best-selling book which explores how history repeats itself.

The Stranger Within (2013). A dark psychological thriller in which a psychiatrist and his wife, played by William Baldwin and Estella Warren, encounter murder and mayhem on a Mediterranean island.

A Long Way Down (2014). Pierce Brosnan and Toni Collette star in this comedy, based on the novel by Nick Hornby, about four people who form a surrogate family to help each other through tough times.

The Night Manager (2016). A popular BBC miniseries based on John le Carre's novel, starring Tom Hiddleston and Hugh Laurie, featuring some stunning Mallorcan landscapes.

ABOUT THIS BOOK

This *Explore Guide* has been produced by the editors of Insight Guides, whose books have set the standard for visual travel guides since 1970. With top-quality photography and authoritative recommendations, these guidebooks bring you the very best routes and itineraries in the world's most exciting destinations.

BEST ROUTES

The routes in the book provide something to suit all budgets, tastes and trip lengths. As well as covering the destination's many classic attractions, the itineraries track lesser-known sights, and there are also ex-cursions for those who want to extend their visit outside the city. The routes embrace a range of interests, so whether you are an art fan, a gourmet, a history buff or have kids to entertain, you will find an option to suit.

We recommend reading the whole of a route before setting out. This should help you to familiarise yourself with it and enable you to plan where to stop for refreshments – options are shown in the 'Food and Drink' box at the end of each tour.

For our pick of the tours by theme, consult Recommended Routes for… (see pages 6 – 7).

INTRODUCTION

The routes are set in context by this introductory section, giving an overview of the destination to set the scene, plus background information on food and drink, shopping and more, while a succinct history timeline highlights the key events over the centuries.

DIRECTORY

Also supporting the routes is a Directory chapter, with a clearly organised A – Z of practical information, our pick of where to stay while you are there and select restaurant listings; these eateries complement the more low-key cafés and restaurants that feature within the routes and are intended to offer a wider choice for evening dining. Also included here are some nightlife listings, plus a handy language guide and our recommendations for books and films about the destination.

ABOUT THE AUTHORS

This edition of Explore Mallorca was updated by Maciej Zglinicki, building on work by Victoria Trott and Tara Stevens. Victoria Trott has updated several guidebooks on the Spanish mainland and Balearic Isles and has travelled extensively in the country. Tara Stevens writes about Spanish lifestyle, food and wine for a wide variety of international publications.

CONTACT THE EDITORS

We hope you find this Explore Guide useful, interesting and a pleasure to read. If you have any questions or feedback on the text, pictures or maps, please do let us know. If you have noticed any errors or outdated facts, or have suggestions for places to include on the routes, we would be delighted to hear from you. Please drop us an email at hello@insightguides.com. Thanks!

CREDITS

Explore Mallorca
Editor: Helen Fanthorpe
Authors: Victoria Trott, Tara Stevens and Maciej Zglinicki
Head of Production: Rebeka Davies
Update Production: AM Services
Picture Editor: Tom Smyth
Cartography: original cartography Berndston & Berndston, updated by Carte
Photo credits: Alamy 40, 45, 71, 121; Bodegas Angel 81, 82, 82/83, 83L; Dreamstime 43, 62; Fotolia 72B; FotoLibra 64/65; Getty Images 1, 4/5T, 8/9T, 84/85T; Greg Gladman/Apa Publications 4MC, 4MR, 4MC, 4ML, 4ML, 4MR, 6TL, 6MC, 6ML, 6BC, 7T, 7M, 7MR, 8ML, 8MC, 8MC, 8ML, 8MR, 8MR, 10, 10/11, 12, 13, 13L, 14, 14/15, 16, 16/17, 18/19, 20/21, 21L, 22, 23, 24, 25L, 26, 28ML, 28MC, 28MR, 28ML, 28MC, 28/29T, 30/31, 32, 32/33, 33L, 34, 34/35, 36, 36/37, 37L, 38, 41L, 41, 42, 44, 46, 46/47, 47L, 48, 48/49, 49L, 50, 50/51, 51L, 52, 53T, 52/53T, 56, 57, 57L, 58/59, 60, 60/61, 61L, 62/63, 66, 68/69, 74, 74/75, 76, 76/77, 77L, 78, 78/79, 84MC, 84ML, 84MR, 84ML, 92/93, 101, 102/103, 104/105, 106, 107, 107L, 108, 109, 111, 112, 113, 113L, 114, 115, 116, 117, 118, 118/119, 120T, 120B; Hotel Bon Sol 87; iStockphoto 18, 25, 28MR, 53M, 55, 58, 97; Leonardo 84MC, 84MR, 89, 91, 99; MNAC 27; Robert Harding 7MR, 20, 67, 68, 70, 72T, 80; Simply Fosh 95; SuperStock 39, 72/73
Cover credits: Shutterstock (main&bottom)

Printed by CTPS – China

Second Edition 2017

DISTRIBUTION

UK, Ireland and Europe
Apa Publications (UK) Ltd
sales@insightguides.com
United States and Canada
Ingram Publisher Services
ips@ingramcontent.com
Australia and New Zealand
Woodslane
info@woodslane.com.au
Southeast Asia
Apa Publications (Singapore) Pte
singaporeoffice@insightguides.com
Hong Kong, Taiwan and China
Apa Publications (HK) Ltd
hongkongoffice@insightguides.com
Worldwide
Apa Publications (UK) Ltd
sales@insightguides.com

SPECIAL SALES, CONTENT LICENSING AND COPUBLISHING

Insight Guides can be purchased in bulk quantities at discounted prices. We can create special editions, personalised jackets and corporate imprints tailored to your needs.
sales@insightguides.com
www.insightguides.biz

INDEX

MAP LEGEND

● Start of tour	★ Place of interest	ⓘ Tourist information	Park
→ Tour & route direction	♠ Statue/monument		Important building
❶ Recommended sight	✉ Main post office		Hotel
❷ Recommended restaurant/café	🚌 Main bus station		Transport hub
	✶ Windmill		Shop / market
	🏰 Castle / ruin		Pedestrian area
			Urban area

INSIGHT ⊙ GUIDES

OFF THE SHELF

Since 1970, **INSIGHT GUIDES** has provided a unique perspective on the world's best travel destinations by using specially commissioned photography and illuminating text written by local authors.

Whether you're planning a city break, a walking tour or the journey of a lifetime, our superb range of guidebooks and phrasebooks will inspire you to discover more about your chosen destination.

INSIGHT GUIDES

offer a unique combination of stunning photos, absorbing narrative and detailed maps, providing all the inspiration and information you need.

PHRASEBOOKS & DICTIONARIES

help users to feel at home, when away. Pocket-sized with a free app to download, they go where you do.

CITY GUIDES

pack hundreds of great photos into a smaller format with detailed practical information, so you can navigate the world's top cities with confidence.

EXPLORE GUIDES

feature easy-to-follow walks and itineraries in the world's most exciting destinations, with our choice of the best places to eat and drink along the way.

POCKET GUIDES

combine concise information on where to go and what to do in a handy compact format, ideal on the ground. Includes a full-colour, fold-out map.

EXPERIENCE GUIDES

feature offbeat perspectives and secret gems for experienced travellers, with a collection of over 100 ideas for a memorable stay in a city.